feng shui
life coach

A GODSFIELD BOOK

feng shui life coach

become the person you've always wanted to be with feng shui

Simon Brown

An Hachette Livre UK Company
www.hachettelivre.co.uk

First published in Great Britain in 2009 by
Godsfield Press, a division of Octopus Publishing Group Ltd
2–4 Heron Quays, London E14 4JP
www.octopusbooks.co.uk
www.octopusbooksusa.com

Distributed in the U.S. and Canada by Octopus Books USA:
c/o Hachette Book Group USA
237 Park Avenue
New York NY 10017

ISBN 978-1-841-81343-1

A CIP catalogue record for this book is available from the British Library

Printed and bound in China

10 9 8 7 6 5 4 3 2 1

contents

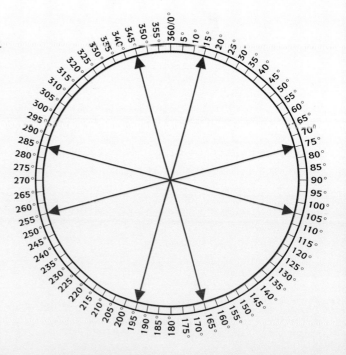

introduction

In this opening section you wil! discover
exactly what feng shui and life coaching
are (see pages 8–11) and how they work
together (see pages 12–19). You will also
find out how to use this book (see pages
20–21) and what makes its approach
special. You will learn about intuition,
conceptual thinking, self-empowerment
and how to use feng shui life coaching
to make deep changes within yourself.
This is the beginning of your exploration
of a new subject that can ultimately
bring about profound change inside you,
enabling you to take on different
challenges and helping you to succeed
where previously you did not.

what is feng shui?

Feng shui is the study of the way in which humans interact with their environment. Over thousands of years, primarily in China and the surrounding countries, a body of knowledge has built up that attempts to explain (and predict) how people feel and behave in certain atmospheres.

feng shui in the modern world

In a practical sense, modern feng shui tends to focus on the place where you live, because your home has the greatest influence on your life in feng shui terms and represents something that you can control. You can also apply feng shui to your working environment, your garden or any space in which you like to spend time. By understanding the vital connection between you and the space in which you live, you can change those things that influence you most — and, as a result, you can change the way you feel.

using your environment for success

Feng shui works on the basis that you have an emotional energy field running through and around your body. The energy can be seen around you as your aura (an energy field surrounding the body that can be photographed, or seen with training) and flows inside your body through activity centres called chakras and out along paths known as meridians. This subtle charge of electromagnetic energy carries your thoughts, ideas and emotions to every cell in your body. The process of charging each cell with your emotional energy is what links your physical and emotional sides. It is a two-way process, so that the way you use your body influences your mind and emotions, and what happens in your mind and to your emotions influences your physical body.

In feng shui thinking, the most important point to understand is that your surface energy mixes with the atmosphere around you, with the result that the changed energy finds its way deep inside your body. This in turn leads on to subtle alterations in the way you think and feel. Therefore, the environment or energy around you can help you experience the kind of emotions that can lead to greater success. At the same time, certain energies in your home could conversely be working against you.

Below: Opening windows and curtains brings in fresh energy, altering how we feel.

Left: Moving furniture to another part of the room places you in a different energy, again influencing your mood.

To summarize, your emotional energy is constantly interacting with the energy around you, so some of your thoughts and feelings will reflect the atmosphere of the place in which you live. Not only that, but your own emotional energy spills out into the rooms you spend time in, filling your environment with your emotions.

putting together the pieces

External influences on your energy fields are many and varied, and include the weather, landscapes, cities, people you live with, homes, work places, the sun's solar energy and the phases of the moon. In addition, the clothes you wear, the food you eat and the people to whom you are physically close can all help you feel different. Feng shui should therefore be seen as just one piece of the jigsaw puzzle of life — and not as the puzzle itself.

Hence, to conclude, your thoughts, feelings and ideas constantly mix with the world around you, so you are always influenced by the combined energies that enter your energy field. At the same time you radiate energy that disperses into the space you occupy.

what is life coaching?

Life coaching is tuition in the art of living: most commonly, helping people do more with their lives. This could be simply making a list at the beginning of each day and systematically working through it, or establishing what you want to do with the rest of your life and finding a new direction.

important

Before you start changing your home with feng shui, it is important to know what you want to achieve. The more specific your aims, the easier it will be to create the ideal atmosphere. The life-coaching part of this book will help you work out how to get the most from feng shui.

self-development challenges

Part of living is taking the skills and talents you have and applying them to make money, enjoy happy relationships and be useful to society. In addition you can seek out challenges that enable you to evolve, at the end of which you may have developed new expertise, benefited from different experiences and as a result become a more interesting, accomplished, well-rounded person.

Right: Giving your home a spring clean refreshes the atmosphere and helps give you a fresh outlook on life.

One of the challenges we all have is to work out is what we need to do between now and the time of our death in order to feel complete, so that we have no regrets at the end of life. Now is the time to start this adventure and, in the biggest sense of the term, life coaching means ultimately being able to know 'I did it all' when it is time to pass on.

On a more superficial level, life coaching could be directed at setting material goals and then organizing yourself to achieve them better; on a deeper level, it could be aimed at investing in yourself to have the experiences, skills, intuition, character traits and emotions to be happy within yourself – wherever you are and regardless of your situation.

make mistakes and learn from them

The quickest way to evolve and develop is to be honest with yourself about your life experiences. There is no good or bad, right or wrong, but you do need an honest appraisal of what you have done and what you can learn from your experiences.

Self-development often comes from making 'mistakes', but a fear of doing the wrong thing can stifle your evolution and cause you to stagnate. Part of life coaching is having the courage and mindset to go out and use such an experience as part of the process of investing in yourself and increasing your inner knowledge of life.

let go of old patterns of behaviour

We all have deep-rooted patterns of behaviour that develop as we grow up. These usually originate from times when we hit on a successful strategy – perhaps being the joker in the school playground in order to win friends. However, as time goes by, these patterns can get in the way of moving forward and becoming someone who adapts in order to succeed in new challenges.

set yourself goals

It can be useful to have some way of measuring yourself as a means to stretch yourself and give your personal evolution greater focus. Aims and goals make it easier to set a challenge and then see if you meet it. If you don't, then you can learn from the experience and discover how to develop in order to achieve your goal next time.

Above: Clean, open spaces free of clutter allow the energy of a room to move more freely, creating a more inspiring atmosphere.

why life coaching and feng shui?

The principles of life coaching and feng shui work naturally together, because applying life coaching to yourself helps you identify what you want out of life, while feng shui helps you work out in what kind of environment you may best succeed.

Below: A money plant, with its smooth, rounded leaves, sends out a very soft energy.

identifying what you want to achieve

Using life-coaching ideas you can be more specific about what you want to achieve with feng shui, and then better able to bring about personal change by immersing yourself in the best type of energy. To understand why, think of yourself as a plant. To help a plant thrive, you need to be aware of what the plant is and what it needs in order to grow. Think of this as the life-coaching component. Then you need to find the ideal soil and light conditions, as well as determine the best time to plant it. You can think of this as the feng shui component of experiencing the atmosphere of a room and the effects of the solar and lunar cycles.

last day meditation
To help decide what you want to achieve, imagine that this is your last day. There is unfortunately the possibility that any one of us could move on to another world suddenly and unexpectedly. If this was your last day, how would you want it to be? What kind of interactions would you want to have with your friends, children, partner, parents? Would you have a meaningless argument on your last day? Would you want to get upset for no real reason?

Choose a quiet room in your home where you have an open space. Sit and contemplate. Watch yourself in imaginary situations behaving the way you would like, rising above the challenges and stresses that life throws up. You may find this easiest when you can be alone and quiet. Try at the beginning of the day to set your mood from the outset.

This is a Zen meditation which can help you to work out how to make the most of your life. Using this technique you can learn to treat each day as though it is your last: to cultivate the kind of interactions with other people and emotions within yourself that would make the day special. By doing this regularly you can emphasize those emotions and characteristics that make each day as worthwhile as possible. One of the benefits of using this is that it helps keep a sense of proportion and

Left: Set up each space in your home so that it has the kind of atmosphere you feel you can best thrive in.

reduce the risk of becoming upset over something which, in the wider context, is not very significant. Would you really want to be upset by a traffic jam, computer problem, misunderstanding at work, children leaving the house in a mess or a disagreement with your lover on your last day? If you learn how to live each day as though it is your last you can free yourself from unnecessary distress and ultimately from filling your body with negative emotions and energy.

feng shui that works on you

The feng shui life-coaching approach differs from ordinary feng shui in that it is directed at *you*. Instead of wanting, for example, a promotion at work and hoping that a feng shui cure will somehow unexpectedly bring it about, the question is: What do I have to change about myself in order to get a promotion? It might be becoming more confident, assertive, inventive, organized, direct or outgoing. Once you have found out what internal change is required, you will learn what kind of energy is most likely to bring this about; you can then introduce more of that energy into the rooms of your home.

the feng shui
life-coaching
process

Identify what you want
to achieve

↓

Discover the internal
change required to bring
it about

↓

Learn what kind of energy
is likely to help achieve this

↓

Introduce more of this
energy into the rooms of
your home

↓

Effect the transformation
that you hoped for

empower yourself with feng shui

The end result of this work is that you become empowered with feng shui life coaching. It happens through you and becomes a tool to help you live your life to the maximum and reach your full potential. This is important, because the more in control you feel, the more likely you are to become the kind of person who can take on challenges in life and grow. Unfortunately, the opposite — hoping that your life will change because of a feng shui cure and believing that power lies in a material object, rather than in you — can be disempowering and enslave you to someone else's ideology.

The idea is that you can make yourself happy — feng shui simply helps that process. The reason why life coaching and feng shui form such a powerful combination is that you are developing yourself through feng shui, rather than hoping it will provide all the answers without making any changes within yourself. By the end of this book you will be able to identify exactly what you want out of life, what you might need to change about yourself to achieve this aim, what kind of atmosphere will help bring about this personal evolution and when will be the easiest time to do so.

change yourself from within

My intention in writing this book is to help you change from within, and to enable you to use feng shui to bring about powerful and lasting alterations that will make it easier to take on challenges and, as a result, evolve and develop your character. You will invest in yourself: you become the end result, the outcome, the achievement. Rather than relying on outside factors, it is the energy *within* you that feng shui will make rich, beautiful and strong.

If you can develop the ability to be happy from within, you can free yourself from the need for external objects in order to gain those feelings. If you can describe how you want to feel inside, I can show you how to create an atmosphere at home that will make it easier to experience those feelings.

translation and transformation

We often think 'If only I had that house [husband/wife/holiday/sum of money/appearance] I would be truly happy.' However, as we all know, there are lots of unhappy people who possess plenty of these things, and happy people with relatively little. It is a mistake to think in terms of absolutes and fixed goals, because these do not necessarily lead to greater happiness and can simply create more stress. You could call this process 'translation' — for example, translating yourself from being unhealthy to healthy, poor to rich, single to married.

The life-coaching dimension of this book explores ongoing 'transformation'. Here there is no beginning or end; it is a process of change and evolution that carries you forward throughout your life. Each day brings something new, and as a result you change and develop. It is the direction and the *way* in which you transform yourself that are important. The more we learn how to transform ourselves, the better we are at doing it as the need arises. You might have goals along the way to give you something to aim at, but they are part of a series of stepping stones and not the end result.

In terms of feng shui, this means understanding your relationship with your environment and being able to use the power of nature effortlessly to continue the process of transformation.

Below: Crisp, clean sheets help refresh your energy when you go to bed and help you to take positive thoughts into your sleep.

evolution and growth

As you evolve and grow, you develop the internal resources to do more with your life and be someone who can take on challenges, such as starting a new business, forming harmonious relationships, writing a book, learning to play an instrument — or whatever it is that takes your fancy. The point is that it is only what goes on inside you that is of interest; what you do with it is secondary.

For example, if you are single and want to be in a relationship, the question is: How do you want to evolve so that you can start a successful relationship? The investment is in yourself and not in the relationship. Feng shui is one way in which you can help bring about profound internal changes by surrounding yourself with a new energy that ultimately nourishes your spirit and soul.

use your intuition

Feng shui life coaching brings a greater awareness and use of your intuition. Intuition is a truly magical attribute, for – without having to reason, think or analyse – your body can automatically tell you what is best for you. This is a subconscious guidance system that helps you do anything from choosing food and knowing whom to trust, to finding a new direction in life. Bypassing your mind in this way removes all the conceptual reasoning that can mislead or constrain you.

We all use feng shui without realizing it — whether it is in choosing the spot for a picnic, preferring a particular seat in a restaurant or arranging the furniture in our homes. We therefore already have our own experience to draw on intuitively when it comes to feng shui. Similarly, we have a lifetime's experience of dealing with challenges and some kind of database on what works and what does not. Life experience forms the basis for intuitive life coaching.

In this book you will learn techniques for greatly enhancing your intuition and how to apply this to the subject of feng shui life coaching. The advantage of this is that if you can sense an atmosphere for yourself you are in a stronger position to base your feng shui on real-life experience. In later chapters you will learn how to feel the energy of a person and a room, and how to work out what you want to do with your life.

You can naturally develop your intuition through creative pursuits such as writing, painting or playing music. Sometimes it is interesting to rely on your intuition for a period of time, just to see where it takes you.

Below: Investing time and devoting energy to yourself means you develop skills that stay with you for ever.

Left: Just being, letting go of learned concepts, can bring a beautiful feeling of freedom and allow your intuition to surface.

the value of concepts

Feng shui is commonly expressed through various concepts, such as yin and yang and the five elements. Man-made concepts, in the form of ideas, principles and theories, are simply clumsy human attempts to explain the world we live in. No concept works all the time in every situation — including those used in feng shui life coaching. When using concepts, it is important to see them for what they are. They are not universal truths; they are thoughts that can help you relate more deeply to a subject, ideas that you can discuss with each other, principles that you can try out in real life to establish when they work best and when they do not. In addition, your conceptual mind can help you to be more empirical, defined and focused in your aims, and through this you may find it easier to develop.

Above: We use feng shui often without realizing it: for example, when choosing a picnic spot.

All the ideas in this book are primarily encouraging you to think, explore, try out and test. I hope they will stimulate you, and will inspire you to discover more about yourself and your relationship with the world around you.

Intuition and conceptual thinking work well together and can provide a necessary balance: if your thinking takes an unhelpful turn, or becomes dogmatic or rigid, then your intuition can pull you back; and should your intuition become confused your rational mind can lead you in a clearer direction.

automatic learning

Simply by reading this book you will have a different perception of the world in which you live. Whether or not you agree with the contents, you will ask questions and as a result you will have changed. How much you change, and in what way, is up to you.

To get the most out of this book I suggest that you read the whole volume quickly, with an open mind. Don't worry if something does not make sense — just keep going. By the end you will see how everything fits together, and it is not until you have finished reading that everything will make sense. As you read through the book, let the words sink into your subconscious naturally. Try to read at times when you feel relaxed and in places that have a tranquil atmosphere.

When you have completed your quick read-through, go back and reread the book more carefully, making sure you fully understand each page before moving on. Some parts may make you want to think about a point for a while; some may make you want to try out the exercises; others may encourage you to make changes to your home. It will all help you understand and develop your knowledge, taking it to a deeper level.

I have designed the book so that you can start straight away and use feng shui practically and safely in your life. On one level, it may all appear very easy; however, the more you apply these ideas and practise feeling energy, and the more you try out feng shui in your home, the more you will discover and, I hope, make the subject your own.

you can do it!

Everything in this book lies within your power. The practices are built around *you*: you are the barometer that will sense the atmosphere of a room; you are the instrument that will feel whether you are evolving to take on the challenges you desire. You do not need any special skills — just the time and awareness to develop your intuition. This is something you will get simply by going about your normal life, except that once you have read the book you will do so with another perception of your relationship to the world you inhabit. In essence, I am asking you to try on a different perception — like a pair of magic glasses that will help you see a different world — and from this decide whether you feel better able to make the most of life.

It is helpful if you can put to one side any fears of making mistakes or any concerns about getting it right, because there are no rights and wrongs in feng shui life coaching. It is really about trying it out: seeing how you feel, learning, and then trying again with another approach if you were not happy with the previous attempt. In this way you will be continually learning through experience and adding to your knowledge of feng shui and life coaching from real life, rather than from abstract ideas created by another person.

how to use this book

I have written this book so that different layers of feng shui and life-coaching information slowly build up, so you need to read through it from the beginning to get the most from it. When reading each section, imagine applying the ideas to your own real-life situation. Think about how you could use the principles in practical ways. It is by playing with the ideas in this book that you will derive most benefit from it and retain the most information. Once you have read the whole book, it then becomes a useful reference tool that you can come back to whenever you need a greater understanding of specific aspects of feng shui and life coaching, or when you want to refer to the various charts to remind you of the different types of energy.

Use your intuition to find somewhere to read this book where you can relax, concentrate and learn.

structure of the book

The next chapter, 'Understanding life coaching', focuses on how you can develop yourself through life coaching, formulating your goals (see pages 32–37) and learning to evolve emotionally (see pages 38–39).

The following part, 'Understanding energy', teaches you how to become more aware of your own energy and of the energy of people and places around you (see pages 42–49); it then goes on to explain the principles of natural environmental energy and the energy of the eight directions (see pages 50–57). You will learn how to relate your own life-coaching goals to each of the eight directions (see pages 58–73) and so begin to explore how to alter your own home to bring about the energetic changes you need. In this section of the book you will also explore the relationship between the atmosphere of a room and the emotions that people living there are most likely to experience; and you will develop ideas on how to be more successful in life by experiencing different emotions through living in a different environment.

'Feng shui life-coaching tools' shows you exactly how you can change your own energy (see pages 76–79). The rest of the chapter then takes you through the process of discovering what the natural energies in your home are and how to map your home according to the energies of the eight directions (see pages 80–89). It also reveals all the ways in which you can change the atmosphere of a room, from the use of colour and different materials to lighting, plants and furniture (see pages 90–113) and explores their influence on your emotions and ultimately on your life. In addition you will discover how the natural cycles of the seasons, the sun and the moon affect your energy (see pages 114–119).

The book concludes with a section on 'Room makeovers with eight-direction energy', which examines the practical application of feng shui life-coaching principles. You will learn the essence of applying the energy of each direction to real-life situations; how to change your home to give it the best atmosphere in which to succeed; and you will be shown makeovers to rooms facing in each of the eight directions (see pages 122–137).

This book will take you on a journey through feng shui and life coaching that will enrich your life and enable you to get more out of it.

Above: To develop your intuition, try sitting in various places with your eyes closed, and 'feel' the atmosphere around you.

understanding life coaching

What do *you* want out of today, this month, this year — or your whole life? Once you have decided, you can work out which emotions will help you to realize your dreams. From there you can establish the best environment for generating those emotions. In these pages you will learn important life-coaching principles (see pages 24–31), including how to overcome past limitations and how to develop a new, positive self-coaching language; you will discover how to set realistic and achievable goals (see pages 32–33) and how to question yourself and develop those goals (see pages 34–37); and you will learn how to evolve emotionally (see pages 38–39).

life-coaching principles

Life coaching is essentially having someone walk through life with you, coaching you to use your mind in a way that will bring about the changes within you that will help you grow and evolve. To give life coaching a focus, the person being coached is encouraged to create aims and goals. The point is not necessarily to achieve those goals, but to use them to identify how you might evolve to meet them. Rather than being a theoretical model, life coaching works best when applied to, and practised in, real-life situations.

what does a life coach do?

You could view life coaching as an exercise or game in which the ultimate outcome is for you to have let go of things that might hold you back from succeeding in life, and to have empowered yourself with new ways of thinking that make it easier to move forward and do what you want with your life.

Right: Another person can be a great mirror for you and help you reflect on how to make the changes you are seeking.

Left: You can use life coaching to help you make the feng shui changes to your home and experience a new energy.

A life coach will work with you on a regular basis to help you create a new image of yourself within which you have the internal resources to be more successful in life. The life-coaching role is non-judgemental and exists primarily to encourage, enthuse, inspire, reassure, support and motivate.

Many of us may not be able to hire a life coach – in which case we can become our own life coach. In this book the life-coaching element is written in terms of working with yourself to bring about your own desired internal changes. Ultimately this becomes empowering, as you know that the resources lie inside you.

use positive language

The life coach within you will speak in a new, positive language in which you feel encouraged and supported. Life-coaching conversations will focus on what you can do and where you feel you have succeeded. Rather than saying that you cannot do something, the life coach within you will assist you in exploring new options for asking for help, developing the skills you need or trying another approach to achieve your goal. With your new mindset you will visualize yourself being the person you want to be – whether that means feeling calm in social situations, saying no to unhealthy foods or creating a living space in which you feel happy.

key life-coaching principles

To become your own life coach, read through the principles listed below and on the following pages, and then apply them to yourself:

- Explore new ways of talking to yourself using positive language

- Find your inner life coach

- Overcome past limitations and failures

- Be honest with yourself

- Listen and indulge in self-reflection

- Identify goals

- Try out new perceptions to deal with fear, doubts and not knowing

- Be open to your own emotional evolution

Right: Use your hands to support and communicate with the part of you that looks after you and keeps you safe.

Practise rewording your thoughts into positive mode. For example, rather than saying 'I cannot keep my home tidy', change this to 'I have not kept my home tidy in the past, but I will spend twenty minutes a day exploring ways to create a tidy home, and this will include doing it myself, researching how I can be more effective and enlisting help.' Before you go to sleep, visualize yourself cleaning your home and enjoying it.

You may find it easier to feel positive in a room that has a sunny, open atmosphere.

your inner life coach

There will be a part of you that will be your own life coach: this could consist of a voice in your head, of feelings or of your own self-image. This will already exist, but may not currently be acting as a life coach and may actually be holding you back and slowing your development. Finding your inner life coach (see below) requires you to work with these parts of yourself so that they transform into a life-coaching role.

exercise: find your inner life coach

You may find this easier to do in a soft, quiet and cosy atmosphere. Use cushions, curtains, fabrics and rugs for greater softness. Try lighting candles and placing them on the floor for a cosier environment. Plenty of plants with soft leaves will contribute to a quieter feel in the room. Try sitting on a big cushion on the floor or lying down on a soft surface, when doing this exercise. If you do this exercise just before you go to sleep, your subconscious will be free to try out your request while you are sleeping.

1 Try to access the part of you that looks after you and keeps you safe. If you feel this part of you has a physical location, put your hand on that part of your body; otherwise, just talk to it. Thank this part of you for looking after you so well and for getting you this far in life; it is helpful if you can feel a genuine sense of gratitude. Ask this part of you if it is willing to listen to options for becoming your personal life coach.

2 Next, wake up the part of you that is creative and inventive — the part that comes up with solutions. Ask it to talk to your protective part about becoming your life coach and exploring working with you in a new way. Then relax and let the two parts of you engage. You might need to do this several times to feel that your inner self is more open to being your life coach.

overcome past limitations and failures

Growing up, we start out being curious, experimental and exploratory. Children constantly test their own boundaries and want to push themselves to the limit. This is natural and part of human development. Initially we are happy to make mistakes because this is how we learn, but in time we think of the outcome of our actions in terms of success or failure. When we discover a limitation or experience that we consider to be a failure, we often use this to create our self-image. We define ourselves as someone who cannot do something because we once 'failed'. This forms part of our protective system and, although it is essential for learning lessons (like not putting your hand in the fire a second time), it can be a strong limiting factor if it prevents us from, say, falling in love if we have had a previous painful experience.

Right: On a piece of paper, write a list of sources of stress: write the reality of each situation on one side and the meaning you have given it on the other. Tear the paper in half to symbolically separate the two.

To move on from what you perceive as past failure and stop the voice in your head that says you cannot do this because you failed before, you need to realize that times change and, just because something did not work before, that does not mean it will not work again. The aim is to learn from your previous experience and ask yourself what you need to do to make it easier to succeed. You may find it easier to do this in a room with a slow, quiet, clean atmosphere.

be honest with yourself

It is all too easy for our minds to spin around making assumptions and to treat what is an opinion as though it were true. Someone says something to us at work and we give it greater meaning than it deserves. We might go on to make the assumption that he or she does not like us or thinks we are not good at our job, when in reality that person had a terrible headache and was in a bad mood.

In nearly all situations stress is self-induced. Something happens and you give it meaning. For example, you might be late for work. Being late is not stressful in itself – it is the meaning you give it that causes the stress. You may assume your colleagues will be annoyed, that you will lose your job or not get promoted. These are self-generated assumptions and, if they cause stress, there is no advantage in thinking like that. The feng shui life-coaching approach is to learn from the experience of being late and then take action to avoid it happening again. This might include visualizing yourself getting up earlier, being quicker in the shower and leaving home earlier. It means being positive about the options for leaving home on time. It might include enlisting the help of a flatmate to be your personal 'leaving on time' trainer.

In any situation, separate out what you have made up in your head from the reality. If you have any thought that is causing you stress or getting in the way of your self-development, ask yourself 'Is this really true?', 'Is there no other way I can think about this?', 'How do I feel when I think like this?' and 'Is there another interpretation that would help me succeed in this situation?'

This can be easier when it is done in an empty, clean and clear space. Try asking yourself these questions in a large room that is reasonably empty of furniture and clutter. You may find it simpler to be clear about the difference between reality and your thoughts when you are in a room with big windows, a high ceiling and one painted in white, light green or pale blue. If you do not have such a room at home, try a museum or art gallery.

Above: A clean and clear space with high ceilings can free your mind to be clear about reality and your thoughts.

Above: Having someone in your life who can be part of your feedback system helps you develop and evolve.

listen to criticism

To succeed in life, you need to have an effective feedback mechanism. You develop by trying something out, assessing the effectiveness of what you did, learning from it, making adjustments and trying again.

If you wanted to learn how to hit a tennis ball over a net, you would try hitting the ball, watch what happens, decide how you wanted to adjust your striking of the ball, try again with the new adjustments, watch and make further changes. Eventually using this method you would get to the point where you could hit the tennis ball so that it skimmed the net and landed where you wanted it to on the other side of the court.

This might seem obvious when learning a sport or new skill, but surprisingly we often turn this mechanism off when it come to other aspects of our lives. We may choose to perceive our feedback system as critical, uncomfortable and negative, instead of providing us with useful information for 'doing better next time'. For certain situations – such as behaviour with other people, the look we create, being intimate with someone, having sex – human beings sometimes confuse the feeling of 'This is who I am' with 'Here is an opportunity to learn and develop'. Our ego gets in the way and we risk arresting our ability to evolve by effectively saying 'I am all right as I am.'

While criticism may simply be someone sounding off because he or she is in a bad mood, if we apply this theory universally we shut out a potentially helpful feedback system. In the feng shui life-coaching approach it becomes important to have people in our lives whom we can trust to provide constructive feedback. These people become an extension of our internal life coach. One word of caution here: it is healthy to engage in relationships where you can develop through external feedback, but not to feel that you are giving away power over your own life to an external life coach; it is more powerful for you to be in control, solicit advice and then decide how to use it.

Below: Writing down reflections on yourself can be therapeutic in itself, and can help you to explore constructive ways to use feedback.

indulge in self-reflection

One challenge is to work out how you can hear and accept useful criticism. A natural human instinct is to become defensive, whereas you might find it better to view criticism as a way to learn and develop yourself. You can try depersonalizing the situation by imagining yourself outside your own body and that the 'imaginary you' is listening to the criticism, absorbing it and learning from it. You can then watch the 'imaginary you' trying out the advice and behaving differently.

This all becomes easier if you do not think in terms of right and wrong, good and bad, or making mistakes. If you go back to the tennis example, all you are doing is hitting a ball and watching where it goes, then hitting the ball differently and seeing where that sends it. There is no right and wrong way – simply an open exploration of the subject. When you apply the same open, non-judgemental attitude to areas of your life that you would otherwise think of as 'good' or 'bad', it becomes simpler to participate in the process of making positive changes in your life.

You may find all this easier to experience when you are in an atmosphere that is open and gentle, but inspiring and stimulating.

identify your goals

One of the key elements in life coaching is developing life goals to work towards. These might be concerned with your career, love life, family or personal development. There are many effective ways to help determine your goals.

exercise: meditate on what you want from life

This approach works by accessing your subconscious, your deepest intuitive part, to look for those life dreams that can ultimately make sure you feel complete and satisfied at the end of your life. When meditating on long-term plans you may find it easier to be out in nature. You could find a special place with which you have a natural affinity, such as by an old tree, next to a lake or under a starry sky. You could also consider a quiet church, museum or gallery. Try meditating just after the new moon and soon after the winter solstice (see pages 118–119) for major realizations.

1 Find a place with a slow, peaceful atmosphere and somewhere comfortable to sit or lie down. Sit facing into the room (if you are inside) and facing a northerly direction, or lie down with the top of your head pointing north.

2 Breathe deeply and slowly, making sure that each part of your body feels physically relaxed.

3 Try to imagine that you are feeling completely satisfied, have a warm feeling in your abdomen and are content. You feel that you have completed everything you want to do and are experiencing a soft happiness. Once you are good at generating these feelings, you can place the emotions in different times, to help you decide what you need to do in order to experience them.

4 Start by imagining that you have reached the end of the day and are feeling incredibly content. Now leave your mind open and let any ideas come to you of what you actually need to do between now and the end of the day to feel this way. As you come out of your meditation, make a note of what is required.

5 When you feel good about meditating on today, try creating a list for the end of the month. Later you can meditate on what you need to do to feel satisfied by the end of the year. Remember to get into the feelings of contentment first. Ultimately you can meditate on what you need to do to feel that way by the end of your life. You can even imagine that you feel happy to move on and leave your body. The biggest question for all of us is: What do I need to do so that in the end I have no regrets, no feelings of 'if only' or 'why didn't I try?' Once you know what you have to do, you have the ultimate life plan and can ensure that you die happy. With all these meditations, keep your mind open and let yourself think freely. There is no right or wrong — just an exploration of your feelings and intuition.

Left: To meditate, find a room where you can sit or lie comfortably and where the atmosphere feels calm.

questionnaire

Another way to identify your goals is through a more conscious processes of asking yourself questions about where you want to be in life and what issues might be holding you back. The questions themselves are important as they can influence what you think about a subject.

key questions for life goals

The wording of these questions is specific and clear. The aim is simple and realistic. Answering these at intervals during the process of change will help you to review it, learn from it and adjust your actions accordingly.

- What would I like to achieve?

- What do I need to do?

- How will I do this?

- When will I do it?

- What is my feedback mechanism?

- How will I learn from the process?

- When will it be completed?

- How will I know when I have succeeded?

how to ask yourself questions

Try to question yourself using words like 'me', 'I', 'my' and 'myself'. Avoid the temptation to generalize or to ask questions of someone else. Your questions should ask you to be quite specific about your objectives – this is important to help you set clear goals.

Set yourself one simple goal at a time. Goals that rely on several achievements can become confused. So, rather than have a general goal of being early for work (which might involve getting up earlier, not wasting time before leaving the house and not stopping for a coffee on the way), initially start with the goal of getting up 20 minutes earlier each day.

Make your goals realistic. The aim is not to achieve grand targets or impress yourself, but to practise working towards a goal and developing yourself in the process. Start with goals that are easy to achieve, so that you can build up your confidence. There is no need to begin with your biggest goal: if your main goal is to lose weight, start with the simple aim of eating fresh fruit instead of foods with added sugar.

Define your goals in ways that are measurable and specific, because you will want to know whether you have succeeded. For example, 'making the bed every day' is measurable, whereas 'keeping the house tidy' is not (it is a matter of opinion).

Set yourself a time in which to achieve your goals, so that they are not open-ended. You might aim to walk for an hour a day for one month; at the end of the month you will know if you have succeeded.

When deciding on your goals, you may find it easiest to achieve in an orderly, neat and uncluttered room.

sample questionnaire

What would I like to achieve? Lose 2 kg (4½ lb) of weight.

What do I need to do? Include in my daily diet one salad, an apple, a carrot, a small head of broccoli, two bean and vegetable soups, a fresh vegetable juice, 1 litre (1¾ pt) of water and steamed fish, instead of eating dairy food, meat, foods with added sugar, bread and soft drinks.

How will I do this? I will only keep in my home the foods I want to eat on my new diet, and will only go to restaurants where I can order the dishes on my new diet.

When will I do it? I will do it every day.

What is my feedback mechanism? I will keep a food diary. I will review this and use it to help me learn from any mistakes.

How will I learn from the process? I will look at why I ate foods I wished to avoid, then take steps to avoid that particular situation or give myself other options, such as taking my own food with me.

When will it be completed? In one month.

How will I know when I have succeeded? I will weigh myself at the beginning and end of the month.

Above: Clear a space, do a few long, slow stretches, breathe deeply and then you can settle down to write out your questionnaire.

develop your goals

Another very effective way to determine your life goals is to explore any issues that you currently find upsetting or that are occupying your thoughts. The issues may seem relatively small, but frequently bigger concerns are hidden by something that seems quite minor.

exercise: develop your goals

Follow the process below to help you establish goals for personal change.

1 Write out the issue that you are upset about.

2 Write down what it means to you, and what your interpretation is.

3 Ask yourself if this is really true – absolutely true. Ask yourself if there is no other way of looking at it. Write down your answers.

4 Write out the issue again, referring only to yourself and, using words like 'me', 'I', 'my' and 'myself', describe your feelings.

5 Ask yourself how you feel about this interpretation. Does it help you to have the emotions you desire?

6 If you are not happy, go back to question 4 and use it to identify a goal that will help you feel differently.

7 Imagine yourself in this situation and make a note of how you feel.

If you are happy with the changes that you suggested in answer 6, you can use these as the basis for your new life goal.

Right: The more honest you are with yourself, the more effective the exercise will be.

sample exercise

Write out the issue that you are upset about. My husband does not spend enough time with me.

Write down what it means to you, and what your interpretation is. I feel that he does not find me interesting or fun to be with.

Ask yourself if this is really true – absolutely true. Ask yourself if there is no other way of looking at it. Write down your answers. I am not 100 per cent sure. He does like his golf a lot, and I choose not to play golf with him.

Write out the issue again, referring only to yourself and, using words like 'me', 'I', 'my' and 'myself', describe your feelings. I feel lonely when I am on my own.

Ask yourself how you feel about this interpretation. Does it help you to have the emotions you desire? I feel low, a bit heavy and withdrawn. I do not enjoy these feelings.

If you are not happy, go back to question 4 and use it to identify a goal that will help you feel differently. My goal is to spend more time with my friends and family; to find things to do that help me feel happy on my own.

Imagine yourself in this situation and make a note of how you feel. I feel lighter, more sociable and I am smiling. I am more enthusiastic about going to a dance class and taking up photography again.

Above: Try not to lose power by attempting to change others – look for changes you can make yourself.

new life goals

• To spend more time with my friends and family

• To find things to do that help me feel happy on my own

emotional evolution

Once you know what you want to do in life, you can explore the state of mind that will best help you achieve your goals. This is an essential step in the process of change, and if it is overlooked it can be hard to move on to a new phase of your life. Imagine going into a potentially successful situation: notice if any emotions get in the way or are missing. If you are looking for a new job, is fear or insecurity stopping you? Do you need greater confidence to impress at your interview? This part of the process is like peeling an onion, as you may have to go through several layers to discover the ultimate emotional change that will bring about significant transformation in your deepest self.

working through the layers

Let's take the example of a woman who is single and wants to start a relationship, but has been unsuccessful. The relevant questions are: Do you meet desirable men? When you meet someone you are interested in, do you make an emotional connection? Do you find it easy to move a good friendship on to something more romantic? Do you sabotage the relationship in the early stages?

Below: Make time to contemplate and slowly work through the emotional layers surrounding an issue.

Once you can identify exactly what the problem is, you can discover what kind of emotional change will make a difference. In this example, if the woman does not meet many desirable men, this might be due to a lack of the various emotions that help her feel outgoing, expressive or adventurous. Or perhaps there might not be enough energy directed at being playful, flirting and fun-loving. If there is difficulty in moving a relationship into something more intimate, it could be due to a lack of emotional energy focused on feeling sensual, tactile or lustful. A tendency to sabotage a promising relationship could be the result of too much emotional energy associated with pride, self-righteousness or being judgemental.

Each person is different, and it is up to you to work through the following steps as honestly as possible. There is nothing to lose by exploring different patterns of behaviour and emotions — and so much to gain. It would be a shame to get attached to emotional patterns that get in the way of being happy in life. It is our willingness to change that most determines our ability to succeed in any situation.

three steps to emotional evolution

1 Think through what you want to do today, this month, this year or in your lifetime.

2 Imagine yourself in that situation, or remember a time when you tried something similar.

3 Take an honest exploration of which emotions are getting in the way of what you want to do, or which emotions you need more of in order to succeed in your specific aim. With this information you can then explore making the appropriate changes to your internal energy.

the emotional evolution process

Below are some examples of how to use the emotional evolution process. Use them to work on yourself, writing down what you would like to change about yourself and then reading through the following section to find out how to change your energy and what alterations to make in your home.

aim	imagined or previous difficulty	emotion or state of mind
To start a new career	Nervous in interviews	Too fearful, lacking confidence and self-belief
To be more sociable and make friends	Feeling shy	Too insecure, not expressive enough, assuming that other people are not interested
To argue less in relationships	Lack of understanding from partner	Too judgemental, not accepting a partner enough, making unhelpful assumptions
To criticize my children less	Wanting them to do well in life	Having unrealistic expectations, needing to be in control, unable to let children learn from their mistakes
To gain greater recognition at work	Not noticeable enough	Too withdrawn, not outgoing enough, lacking pride
To feel less stressed	Pressure of deadlines and meetings	Too intense, not flexible enough, high expectations, unable to see the bigger perspective

understanding energy

Now that you have defined some goals to work towards, you can begin to explore the connection between your thoughts, your feelings, your energy and the energy all around you. This part of the book will help you first to sense your own energy (see pages 42–43) and that of others (see pages 44–45). It will then enable you to understand the energy of a room (see pages 46–47), the energy around you (see pages 48–49) and the energy of the natural world (see pages 50–57), as well as the psychological energy of the eight directions (see pages 58–73).

sensing internal energy

The following exercises will help you develop your sensitivity to energy in yourself, in other people and in your environment. The more sensitive you become, the more fine-tuned your feng shui work will be — you will be superbly attuned to your own needs and to those of your friends and family.

exercise: how to feel energy in your hands

In this exercise you work on feeling energy between your hands. Later you will use the same skill to sense the energy of a room. Signs of energy in your hands can be a tingling sensation in your palms, a feeling of entering and pulling apart, a field of warmth or a magnetic sensation as you change direction, moving your palms towards and away from each other.

1 Wear loose cotton clothing, and find a space that has a natural atmosphere: a big room or a secluded space outdoors. You may get the best results when doing this barefoot outside at sunrise so that you can feed off the rising energy from the earth.

2 Stand and rub your palms and the backs and sides of your hands vigorously together until they are warm. Rub the outside of your arms, stimulating the flow of energy to your palms.

3 Stretch upwards while breathing out. Stretch your head to each side. Repeat this until you feel relaxed from your head and chest to your hands, allowing energy to flow freely.

Left: The easiest way to feel the energy used in feng shui is between your palms.

4 Vigorously shake your hands, keeping your wrists and fingers loose. Imagine that you are shaking your blood down to the tips of your fingers.

5 Hold the base of your thumb firmly with your other thumb and index finger and massage along to your thumbnail. Squeeze each side of the nail, inhale and quickly pull your thumb and index finger away from your other thumb as you exhale. Imagine that you have a multicoloured flame of energy around your thumb and that you are extending this. Repeat with each finger on the same hand, and then with the other hand.

6 Put your palms together in front of your neck. As you breathe in, imagine that you are breathing a powerful colour, feeling or sound into your body. As you breathe out, imagine the powerful energy moving into your hands. Repeat at least six times.

7 Dry your palms and rub them together vigorously. Hold your hands about 2.5 cm (1 in) apart and then move them closer and further apart. Be sensitive to any feeling in your palms. Repeat with your hands further apart. Try doing this very slowly, slightly quicker, at very small distances and with larger movements.

8 As you bring your hands close together, you may feel the palms getting warmer. Moving them away, it may feel as though you are pulling this warm energy field apart. You may sense a slight magnetic sensation between your hands. If you do not feel anything at first, keep trying, because the more you do this exercise the more sensitive you will become.

ways to access your inner energy

- Eat wholefoods that are high in living energy. This includes vegetables, fruit, wholegrains, dried beans, nuts, seeds and fermented foods.

- Wear clothing made from natural materials.

- Work, relax or sleep at least 1 m (3¼ ft) from electrical equipment.

- Make sure that your bedding is made of pure cotton and that your home contains as many natural materials as possible.

- Practise Tai Chi, Chi Kung or yoga.

- Do the exercise described on the left, daily.

- Walk barefoot whenever possible, to connect with the energy of the earth.

Left: Sleeping on natural materials and away from electrical equipment improves your energy flow.

sensing the energy
of other people

You can work with another person to develop your skills in sensing energy. This takes a bit of time and practice, but is well worth the effort involved.

exercise: healing the energy of the back

This exercise helps you to feel energy in terms of hot and cold, and to feel how strong energy is on the surface of the body.

1 Ask a friend to lie on his front with his back exposed. Move your hand slowly across his back about 2.5 cm (1 in) from his skin. Locate and note areas that feel hotter or cooler than the rest.

2 To confirm where the energy is in excess or deficient, drag the back of your thumbnails slowly and firmly down either side of your friend's spine. Watch his back carefully and you will see two red lines appear. Some areas will display a broad line, others a thin line or may not even turn red at all. A broad, strong red line indicates plenty of energy coming to the surface; a thin line suggests weaker energy.

3 Place your hands gently on the weaker areas, and imagine that you are breathing energy into your friend's back with each out-breath.

4 After three minutes, lift your hands slightly and see if you can feel a magnetic sensation between your hands and his back. Keep your hands close to the same area of your friend's back until you feel greater heat in your hands. Then move your hands away slowly. Your friend may still feel as if your hands are on his back even though you have removed them.

5 When healing is complete, repeat the test with your thumbnails. You should see a more even line as the energy radiates more harmoniously.

Above: Rest your hands gently and breathe energy into cooler parts of the back.

exercise: sensing the flow of energy

Once you can feel the energy between your own hands and on a friend's back, you can move on to sensing the *flow* of energy.

1 Ask a friend to lie on her front. Place her hands on the base of her spine and pull them evenly and gently. Look to see if the hands are evenly aligned. If not, massage her shoulders and try again. Lay her hands on the surface she is lying on.

2 Now move one of your hands up and down her back (close to the skin but without touching), with your palm facing in the direction in which you are moving your hand. So, as your hand moves up the back, your palm faces your friend's head, and as you move down you turn your palm to face her feet. As you move your hand, be aware of a slight resistance in one direction. This indicates that you are moving against the flow of energy, and that your friend's energy is moving in the opposite direction.

3 To confirm this, move your hand vigorously several times in the direction that it moved when you felt resistance. Now you might feel that the direction of energy flow has changed. Check by placing your friend's hands at the base of her spine again. In most people you will find that one arm appears longer.

4 Vigorously push your friend's energy back in the original direction. Recheck her arm lengths — you will probably find they are similar again. The aim is to feel the direction in which your friend's energy is flowing. You may need to try this many times on different people before you feel confident about the process.

Below: See if you can feel a slight resistance while moving your hand.

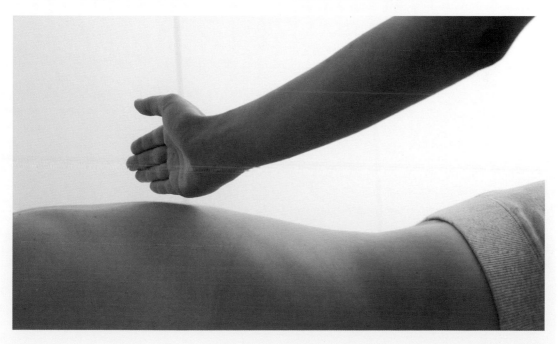

sensing the energy of a room

You can feel the energy of a room, just as you can feel the energy between your own hands and across someone's back. It is useful to be able to do this, because then you can sense for yourself where in the home there is more energy and which way it is flowing.

exercise: up-and-down and sideways energy

The easiest way to start to feel the energy of a room is to sense whether the energy is moving up or down. In a typical room the strongest energy flow will be in the corners, at the edge of a window or near a door, because there is often greater turbulence here.

1 Start by freeing up your neck, shoulders and back. Rub, clap and massage your hands to ensure that you are relaxed and that your own energy is flowing freely and easily.

2 Choose a corner, window or door and stand so that you can raise and lower your outstretched hand easily. Lift your hand with your palm turned up and then, as you lower it, turn your hand over so that your palm faces the floor. Move your arm slowly so that it takes about two seconds to raise your hand and another two to bring it down again. Position yourself so that your hand moves close to the wall; if you do not feel anything in one place, try other parts of the room (or another room).

3 As you raise and lower your hand, be sensitive to any slight resistance against your palm in one direction. If you feel a little resistance in one direction, then the energy will be flowing against your hand. So, if you feel resistance against your palm as you lift your hand, the energy in that part of the room is flowing downwards. Conversely, if you feel resistance as your hand moves down, the energy in that part of the room is flowing upwards. In some places you will feel the energy easily in the palm of your hand, indicating an intense, strong flow; in other places you may find it hard to feel anything, suggesting a thinner, more dispersed, slower-moving energy.

4 Once you have mastered sensing the up-and-down flow of energy, you can try feeling the energy flowing horizontally, by moving your hands sideways, remembering to turn your palm over as you change direction.

5 Also, try feeling the flow of energy in various public buildings. Sometimes older buildings have a stronger energy flow, and you might find that the corner of an old church or beneath a skylight in a museum has a strong flow of vertical energy.

6 Once you get to know a room in terms of its energy, try feeling the energy at different times of day and with different people in it, to sense how the flow changes. You will also be able to use this skill to test the feng shui recommendations that come later in this book.

sensing the energy around you

One of the aims of feng shui life coaching is to turn you into an energy-sensing being. You already do this to a greater or lesser extent, but the goal is to bring into your conscious mind the ability to sense energy, so that you become a barometer for the kind of energy that is present wherever you are.

creating awareness

You should be able to consciously sense the energy in a place, note your thoughts and your mood, then look for clues that explain why the energy feels the way it does. You should also practise feeling the energy with your hands to confirm your overall impressions.

Right: In this tall cathedral it would be interesting to feel the energy close to the columns.

For example, you might sit in a hotel lobby and feel restless. Feel the energy around you with your hands. If it feels intense, you know that you are seated in a path of fast-flowing energy. Look around to see if there is any reason for this. Is it due to a protruding corner, a long mirror, a shiny floor, a row of doors or the movement of people?

Try different types of environment. Compare your thoughts and emotions when sitting in a huge museum, a gallery, a cathedral, a mosque, a temple or a synagogue with the feelings you experience in a small, crowded café. Check the energy flow to establish what type of energy leads to those internal feelings, then look for what it is about the building, decoration and people that you think contributes to that energy flow and your current mood.

As you develop this new awareness, you will be creating a database of experience with different atmospheres and how they affect you. In addition, you will be developing a real-life knowledge of what it is about a building that produces certain atmospheres. This is the essential ingredient for becoming intuitive with feng shui. With this internal library, you will be able to know instinctively how to create the best environment for you to succeed in. As we look at the feng shui concepts and ideas on the following pages, you will be able to correlate these with your own experience and, through this, explore the concepts in a way that is real to you.

set yourself goals

I suggest that you give yourself the following goal: once a week go to a different public building: a café, restaurant, museum, gallery, library, hotel lobby, workplace or shopping mall. Find somewhere to rest and relax. After 15 minutes write down your thoughts, feelings and mood. Describe the atmosphere you sense in this place. Look around and make a note of any features you think contribute to this: is it the colours, the plants, the lighting, the materials used on the floor, the shape of the space, the windows and natural light, the size of the space, the furniture, the people, the art or the open space?

Be aware that in certain places you might feel that your thoughts and emotions are unhelpful. It is important to recognize what kind of energy appears to be contributing to this. Could it be too slow, fast, thin, condensed, volatile, consistent or moving too strongly in a particular direction?

energy descriptions

Throughout this book energy is described in terms of direction, speed, density and volatility. These are our real-life experiences of energy, and we can use these terms as a way to express the actual flow of energy in a room.

- Direction: Up, down, outward, inward, multi-directional (flowing easily around the body)

- Speed: Fast, steady, slow

- Density: Concentrated, even, thin

- Volatility: Volatile (liable to change rapidly), fluid, consistent

natural environmental energy

In feng shui we strive to understand how the environmental energy or atmosphere around us will affect us in terms of directions, times of day and seasons. The principle behind this is that, as the sun moves through the sky during the day, it charges up a building from different directions with its solar energy.

Above: The setting sun sends energy into the western part of this house.

directional energy

In a typical day in the northern hemisphere the following occurs:

- The sun will rise in the east and will first energize the eastern side of your home.
- During the morning the sun will ascend through the sky, energizing the south-eastern side of your home.
- At midday the sun will reach its highest point and energize the southern side of your home.
- During the afternoon the sun will descend in the sky, energizing the south-western part of your home.
- During sunset and the start of evening the sun will energize the western part of your home.
- In the summer the sun will rise in the north-east and set in the north-western, bringing its energy to all these parts of your home.

If you live in the southern hemisphere, north and south are reversed: so the sun rises in the east, ascends in the north-east, reaches its full height and strength in the north, then starts to descend in the north-west and sets in the west.

time and seasonal energy

In feng shui the type of energy is named by the direction (see above). So the kind of energy that you experience at sunrise is called eastern energy, because this is where the sun is at that time. To make the experience more powerful, you can include the cycle of environmental energy through the year. Different directions can be associated with different times of the day and year. So now the energy in the eastern part of your home is said to be similar to the energy of the sunrise and the spring. This is an essential link to be able to ascertain each type of energy for yourself.

northern-hemisphere time and season associations

direction	time	month	season	aspect of nature
North	Midnight	December	Winter	Water
North-east	Early morning	January, February	Winter changing to spring	Mountain
East	Sunrise	March	Spring	Thunder
South-east	Morning	April, May	Spring changing to summer	Wind
South	Midday	June	Summer	Fire
South-west	Afternoon	July, August	Summer changing to autumn	Earth
West	Sunset	September	Autumn	Lake
North-west	Evening	October, November	Autumn changing to winter	Heaven

southern-hemisphere time and season associations

direction	time	month	season	aspect of nature
South	Midnight	June	Winter	Water
South-east	Early morning	July, August	Winter changing to spring	Mountain
East	Sunrise	September	Spring	Thunder
North-east	Morning	October, November	Spring changing to summer	Wind
North	Midday	December	Summer	Fire
North-west	Afternoon	January, February	Summer changing to autumn	Earth
West	Sunset	March	Autumn	Lake
South-west	Evening	April, May	Autumn changing to winter	Heaven

compass associations

Using the information in these charts, you can experience the time of day and year to get a real-life feeling of each kind of energy. You can see that this cycle is built around the four main compass directions and times of year. In the northern hemisphere these are as follows:

- East = 20 or 21 March = spring equinox
- South = 20 or 21 June = summer solstice
- West = 22 or 23 September = autumn equinox
- North = 21 or 22 December = winter solstice

For the southern hemisphere, simply reverse the table above. The other four directions relate to the changing times in between.

natural connections

The Chinese also gave each type of environmental energy a connection with an aspect of nature, to further describe the energy in terms that you can go out and experience for yourself. These natural images actually come from the trigrams (a series of three parallel lines) used in the *I Ching* — or *Book of Changes*, one of the oldest Chinese classic texts, which employs a system of divination to offer insights into a reader's situation — and consist of water, mountain, thunder, wind, fire, earth, lake and heaven. To have a real-life experience of heaven, think of looking at the stars and the cosmos at night.

let nature empower you

The aim is that you can associate each direction with the relevant times of day, season and aspect of nature, then apply this information to describe each energy using your real-life experience of nature. This will bring you closer to understanding how different kinds of energy can effect your emotions and behaviour. Once you appreciate this, you can bring more of certain kinds of energy into your body to help bring about deep, profound and lasting changes. Most commonly this will be achieved by changing the energy inside your home.

The more you can experience nature in all its different forms, the more real and a part of you your understanding of feng shui will be. This reduces the risk of being enslaved to someone else's concepts, and increases your ability to be empowered by the subject and make it part of your life philosophy.

Below: Meditating as the sun rises close to the spring equinox would help you feel eastern energy.

the energy of each direction

Based on these associations and the times of day and season, we can write out words to describe the energy of each direction. The following is a personal interpretation based on my experience of each energy. If your experience is different, you can add your own words. I have included the energy flow in terms of direction, speed, density and volatility. The directions are for the northern hemisphere, the southern hemisphere's are in brackets.

north (south)
Associations Winter, night, water
Key words Flexible, quiet, dark, flowing, moonlit, starry, mysterious, tranquil, regenerative
Energy flow Multi-directional, slow, thin, fluid

north-east (south-east)
Associations Winter/spring, early morning, mountain
Key words Crisp, clean, clear, sharp, quick, hard, cold
Energy flow Multi-directional and up, fast, concentrated, fluid

east
Associations Spring, sunrise, thunder
Key words New, fresh, loud, temporary, electric, active, beginning
Energy flow Up, fast, concentrated, fluid

south-east (north-east)
Associations Spring/summer, morning, wind
Key words Rising, growing, changeable, persistent, spreading, moving
Energy flow Up, fast, even, fluid

south (north)
Associations Summer, midday, fire
Key words Hot, bright, radiant, expansive, shimmering, vibrant
Energy flow Outward, fast, thin, volatile

Above: The reflective quality of a lake suggests western energy and encourages self-reflection.

south-west (north-west)
Associations Summer/autumn, afternoon, earth
Key words Descending, settling, earthy, warm, waning, soft, ripening
Energy flow Down, steady, even, fluid

west
Associations Autumn, sunset, lake
Key words Contracting, completed, harvested, reflective
Energy flow Inward, steady, concentrated, consistent

north-west (south-west)
Associations Autumn/winter, evening, heaven
Key words Prepared, looking down, ending, diminishing, closing down
Energy flow Inward, slow, concentrated, consistent

experiencing natural environmental energy

To try out each type of environmental energy for yourself, make a point of visiting the appropriate locations at the times when that energy is most prevalent. So, for example, you could climb a small mountain or go skiing before sunrise in January or February to experience north-eastern energy in the northern hemisphere (south-eastern energy in the southern hemisphere).

how to experience environmental energy

Opposite are some suggestions for how to experience the environmental energy of each direction. Once you are in your desired location, try to relax and be aware of how you feel. Carefully observe the nature around you and look for clues as to how the energy is created. Use yourself and your emotions, thoughts and moods as a barometer for the energy. The directions are based on the northern hemisphere, with the southern hemisphere's equivalent in brackets.

Below: A strong wind refreshes our emotional energy and helps experience south-eastern energy.

north (south)

Suggested activity Go out into nature at night in December (June). Pick a clear night so that you can see the stars and the universe above you. Be close to water — whether sea, lake or river. Alternatively choose a night when ice or water is lying on the ground.

Potential emotion You might be deeply aware of yourself and yet at the same time conscious of the vastness of the cosmos. You may experience a stillness, peace and tranquillity.

north-east (south-east)

Suggested activity Try being a mountainous region in January or February (July or August) and going outside very early in the morning before the sun rises. Ideally the atmosphere will be cold, crisp and hard.

Potential emotion Be aware of any feelings of clarity, decisiveness or motivation.

east

Suggested activity Walk barefoot on the grass to feel the dew rise in March (September) and watch the sunrise. Even better, experience a thunderstorm.

Potential emotion You may feel the energy rise around you. Note your feelings at the beginning of the day. You might feel enthused and ready to move forward into the new day. Note the electric excitement of a storm.

south-east (north-east)

Suggested activity Walk on a windy April or May (October or November) morning. Experience the movement and the buffeting.

Potential emotion Be aware of the morning energy, and watch nature as she spreads seeds and activates the environment. Note any sensations of stimulation. See if fresh, new ideas blow into your head.

south (north)

Suggested activity Relax in the midday sun in June (December) and be aware of the flowers in bloom, the colours, radiant heat, brightness and activity.

Potential emotion Be conscious of your own energy moving to the surface. Perhaps you also feel more expressive, outgoing and sociable.

south-west (north-west)

Suggested activity Walk with the soil underfoot in the afternoon during July or August (January or February) and be aware of the sun setting. Note the fruits ripening on the vine, and nature moving from growth to sweetness.

Potential emotion You may feel cosy, comfortable, secure or even like having a nap.

west

Suggested activity Sit by a lake so that you can watch the sun set over the water in September (March), and note the sun contracting as she dips below the horizon.

Potential emotion Be aware of end-of-the-day feelings, and see if they bring sensations of contentment or satisfaction. Is there a sense of joy or pleasure?

north-west (south-west)

Suggested activity Walk in the evening under a clear sky. Be aware of the moon and stars. Try to get a sense of looking down at yourself. You can reflect on the day that you have just lived.

Potential emotion You might get a different perspective on life, or feel that you can make new plans for tomorrow.

emotional
environmental energy

This is where you connect different environmental energies with your own emotions, thinking, state of mind or behaviour, writing down words that describe how each energy affects you. This is the key to making personal life changes through feng shui. Again, it is an individual experience. Not only do different people react differently, but the same person's reactions to a room can very widely from one day to the next.

desirable and undesirable emotions

Although everyone will experience environmental energies differently, we can generalize to get ideas on how people might feel in most situations when immersed in each kind of energy, then use this as a starting point for discovering our own unique reactions. Opposite I have described both desirable and undesirable feelings, which I assume people might seek or avoid at different times in their lives (the words in brackets are clues showing where my suggestions come from), based on the appropriate time of day, season and aspect of nature. When you have greater experience of this, you can write out your own real-life interpretations of each type of energy, using this as a template. The directions are based on the northern hemisphere, with the southern hemisphere's equivalent in brackets.

Right: Being aware of your mood in different environments helps you to understand the links between a room's energy and the emotions it provokes.

north (south)

Desirable emotions Peaceful (night), quiet (winter), tranquil (still water), objective (stars), artistic (night), having big vision (stars), affectionate (night), regenerative (soil in winter), healthy (sleep), healing (sleep), sexy (night), conceiving (seeds/dark/winter), mysterious (dark)

Undesirable emotions Lonely (frozen winter), isolated (frozen winter), cold (winter), fearful (dark)

north-east (south-east)

Desirable emotions Clear-minded (mountain), motivated (early morning), decisive (winter/spring mountain), shrewd (early morning), competitive (winter/spring new life), sharp (mountain peaks), quick (early morning), crisp (winter/spring)

Undesirable emotions Obsessive (winter/spring fighting for life), selfish (early morning), critical (mountain looking down)

east

Desirable emotions Ambitious (sunrise), assertive (spring), loud (thunder), active (spring), enthusiastic (sunrise), getting started (morning), confident (thunder)

Undesirable emotions Impatient (spring), irritable (thunder), angry (thunder), rushing (morning)

south-east (north-east)

Desirable emotions Creative (spring/summer), imaginative (wind), communicative (wind), spreading ideas (wind), upward (morning), forward-thinking (morning and spring/summer), growing (spring/summer)

Undesirable emotions Spaced out (wind), distracted (wind), unfocused (gusts of wind), overly analytical (upward morning energy)

south (north)

Desirable emotions Fiery (fire), passionate (hot summer), emotional (turbulent fire), expressive (outward), radiant (outward), social (summer), outgoing (summer), quick-minded (fire), warm (midday and summer), open (outward), entertaining (fire), noticeable (flowers in bloom)

Undesirable emotions Stressed (fire), argumentative (fire), agitated (fire)

south-west (north-west)

Desirable emotions Settled (afternoon), down-to-earth (downward), grounded (earth), practical (earth), adding quality to life (summer/autumn fruits ripening), cosy (afternoon), comfortable (afternoon), making the most of what you have (summer/autumn fruits ripening)

Undesirable emotions Slow (afternoon), dull (downward), energy waning (summer/autumn)

west

Desirable emotions Complete (sunset), satisfied (autumn harvest), joyous (end of working day), pleased (beginning of evening), reflective (lake), romantic (sunset), having inner strength (inward energy)

Undesirable emotions Depressed (inward), withdrawn (inward), inward-looking (inward)

north-west (south-west)

Desirable emotions Dignified (heaven), prepared (evening), responsible (heaven), wise (heaven), experienced (end of year/day), organized (evening), authoritative (end of year/day), showing leadership (heaven), respectful (heaven), showing integrity (heaven), honest (heaven)

Undesirable emotions Judgemental (heaven), having unrealistic standards (heaven), intimidating (heaven)

the psychological energy of the north

Now that you have learned to tune into the energy in and around you, it is time to begin to match the eight directions with your life-coaching goals. Remember the basic qualities of the energy of the north (see page 53). You can experience this energy by going outside at night in December in the northern hemisphere (June in the southern hemisphere). The more you experience this energy, the easier it becomes to know when you need it and how it can help you in life.

northern energy characteristics

- Tranquil

- Objective

- Artistic

- Meditative

- Having a big vision

- Healing

- Sexy

- Lonely

- Fearful

understanding northern energy

Here are some ideas to get you started on learning the emotions of this energy, in terms of the way you may want to feel and some feelings that you may want to avoid.

tranquil
The quiet atmosphere of the night and winter combines to make northern energy ideal when you want to feel at ease, peaceful or able to relax completely and unwind.

objective
As the tranquil atmosphere of the north removes many distractions and can help you feel emotionally and mentally calm, it becomes easier to step back and look at your life more objectively.

artistic
Because the night is an unnatural time for humans to be active, working in this atmosphere can bring interesting and unusual thoughts, making it a helpful energy for feeling original and different.

meditative
The still, dark atmosphere of the north is ideal for feeling meditative and able to look deep into your own soul. This is a helpful environment for self-reflection and contemplation.

having big vision
The large, starry night sky is excellent for engendering a big vision on life and for finding a different perception of who you are and what you want to do with the rest of your life in this universe.

healing

The peaceful energy of the north is helpful for recuperation and regeneration. In this atmosphere you will find it easier to rest and let go of issues that cause stress and anxiety. The north is associated with water, and natural, clean water is considered to have healing properties.

sexy

The energy of the north is considered supportive for sex and conception. In nature it is this dark, night, winter atmosphere that is ideal for seeding and — in terms of humans — for reproduction.

lonely

Too much northern energy can in some people increase the risk of feeling lonely and isolated. This quiet, cold energy may make it harder to feel outgoing and make the effort to meet people and keep existing relationships alive.

fearful

The cold, damp, dark energy can sometimes induce feelings of fear, anxiety or insecurity, if there is excessive northern energy in a home. This atmosphere can make it harder to reach out for help and express your feelings and concerns.

northern energy goals

Examples of goals to work with northern energy include:

- To write a page of freestyle creative writing each day

- To compose a poem each week

- To meditate for ten minutes daily

- To practise stepping back from arguments

- To spend a day each month painting

Left: A northern part of your home could be conducive to creative pursuits such as painting.

the psychological energy of the north-east

Remember the basic qualities of the energy of the north-east (see page 53). Try to experience this energy by going outside before dawn in January and February in the northern hemisphere (July and August in the southern hemisphere), so that you can feel it for yourself.

north-eastern energy characteristics

- Clear-minded
- Motivated
- Decisive
- Shrewd
- Competitive
- Sharp
- Quick
- Obsessive
- Selfish
- Critical

understanding north-eastern energy

Below is a list of emotions that this energy typically brings about. Use it to try and identify the north-eastern energy within you. Remember that it is a helpful energy when you are thinking of a new direction in life.

clear-minded

This fresh, early-morning mountain energy helps clear the mind, creating the space for more considered thinking and fresh new ideas.

motivated

North-eastern energy is considered ideal for motivation, as it has that early-morning, get-up-and-go side to it. The months given above are highly motivating ones in nature, when plants are replenishing their energies and preparing to establish themselves again.

decisive

The cold, crisp, piercing north-easterly winds in the northern hemisphere help you feel less cluttered mentally and make it easy to focus on an issue that requires a solution. This is most helpful when you need to make quick decisions or come to a conclusion about something you have been struggling with.

shrewd

North-eastern energy is particularly helpful when you need to be quick-witted and shrewd. This could apply to making investments, trading or work. The idea is that this energy gives you the ability to spot an opportunity and go for it, without distractions.

competitive

The speed, sharpness and focus of this energy make it ideal for being competitive. With this energy running through your body, you can put more effort into winning than other people can manage.

Left: A white room can help to create the crisp January/February feel of the north-east.

sharp

The energy of the north-east is supportive when you want to simplify your life and get rid of things that no longer work for you. With this energy you may find it easier to let go of emotional attachments to things, and be better able to bring to a conclusion matters that have been dragging on.

quick

The rocky, mountain aspect of this energy helps you feel quick and reactive. With this energy you can feel alive and responsive to situations.

obsessive

Too much north-eastern energy can in some people lead to obsessive behaviour. Typically this would be directed at work, but could also come out in addictive behaviour and a love of gambling. Generally north-eastern energy is not relaxing, so, if you are already feeling stressed, avoid exposing yourself to it.

selfish

People with a lot of north-eastern energy can appear selfish and quick to grab everything for themselves. In this respect it does not always make for good relationships.

critical

North-eastern energy can lead to being critical of others and quick to point out their failings. This can spoil relationships at home and work.

north-eastern energy goals

Examples of goals to work with north-eastern energy include:

- To be motivated to work through a list of three items weekly that you have put off

- To become decisive and take the initiative at least once a day

- To write out your long-term aims for the rest of your life and update them each month

- To play sports or go to the gym once a week

the psychological energy of the east

Try to recall the basic qualities of the energy of the east (see page 53). You can experience this energy by going outside for the sunrise in March in the northern hemisphere (September in the southern hemisphere).

eastern energy characteristics

- Ambitious
- Assertive
- Active
- Enthusiastic
- Getting started
- Confident
- Impatient
- Irritable
- Angry
- Loud

Understanding eastern energy

Here is a list of emotions that eastern energy promotes. Look to see if you recognize any of these traits in yourself, and gauge how much eastern energy you have.

Ambitious
This upward, fresh energy can encourage feelings of ambition. It is a youthful energy that captures a sense of invincibility and is epitomized by the growth of new spring plants. Eastern energy can engender a sense of adventure.

Right: The start of a new day and a new adventure captures the energy of the east.

assertive

The thundery aspect of eastern energy makes it helpful for feeling assertive and able to stand up for yourself. It can be an intimidating force, but – if used wisely – it may help you win respect.

active

Because eastern energy carries the vitality of spring, it is a welcome energy to take in when you want to be more active and get on with life. This is ideal when you feel flat, uninterested or lazy.

enthusiastic

The upward, vital, electric energy of the east is supportive when you want to feel more enthusiastic about life. It is most useful when you need to freshen yourself up and look at life with more eager eyes.

getting started

Since the east is associated with the beginning of the day, it is an energy that helps start new projects, initiate action and find new things to do. You can use it to help you begin a job, career or business.

confident

Bringing a wealth of eastern energy into your own energy field will help you feel confident and will boost your self-esteem. With this springtime energy rising through your body, it becomes easier to believe in yourself and encourages you to feel that you can do things.

impatient

This fast-moving energy can lead to feelings of impatience. You may find that you have a desire to move forward in life quickly, and find it difficult to work with people who are taking a slower approach.

irritable

Strong surges of rising energy can risk making you feel snappy and ill at ease. An excess of this energy, might make you curt and brusque.

angry

The dramatic, thundery nature can set the scene for tantrums and angry outbursts when there is an excess of eastern energy running through your being. Like a storm, however, the energy subsides quickly.

loud

The upward, adventurous energy combined with the imagery of thunder makes eastern energy encourage loud, noisy, boisterous behaviour. Sometimes a person with an abundance of this energy is making too much noise to hear anyone else.

eastern energy goals

Examples of goals to work with eastern energy include:

- To start a new challenging project each spring

- To get up early and go out into nature for half an hour each morning

- To do 20 minutes of exercise and stretching each day

- To learn to cook one new healthy dish each week

the psychological energy of the south-east

Remember the basic qualities of the energy of the south-east (see page 53).
To experience this energy, go outside in the morning in April or May in the northern hemisphere (October or November in the southern hemisphere).

south-eastern energy characteristics

- Creative
- Imaginative
- Communicative
- Upward
- Growing
- Spaced out
- Distracted
- Overly analytical
- Sensitive

Understanding south-eastern energy

Here are some of the feelings that this energy engenders. Read through and consider whether this is something you might want more of or wish to reduce within you.

creative

This morning, spring energy can be stimulating and invigorating, and can help energize the mind into new and creative thinking. Visualize the wind stirring up the deepest recesses of your brain.

imaginative

The imagery of a big, blue morning sky on a windy day is associated with the idea of feeling imaginative and capturing the sensation that anything can happen. The rising spring energy helps energize the mind so that new ideas flow easily.

communicative

The image of the wind blowing seeds across the land is one that associates south-eastern energy with communication. Any means of planting your thoughts into other people's minds — whether through writing, talking, painting, singing, acting or filming — is enhanced with this energy.

upward

The rising springtime, morning energy helps move energy up your body, leaving you feeling more enthusiastic. It is the kind of energy that helps you accomplish a lot without feeling that you really had to exert yourself.

growing

In nature the spring is a time of active growth, and this energy helps your personal growth. It can also encourage you to take on building a business or expanding your range of activities.

south-eastern energy goals

Examples of goals to work with south-eastern energy include:

- To learn to play a musical instrument and spend 20 minutes a day practising

- To go out and take at least ten interesting photographs each week

- To make a short home film each month

- To take singing lessons and join singing events each month

spaced out

The great and varied mental stimulation that this energy encourages can, in excess, lead some people into daydreaming and generally feeling spaced out and unable to focus.

distracted

Too much south-eastern energy can be distracting and there is a risk that you will not actually achieve anything with it. Perversely, some people find it helpful for multi-tasking.

overly analytical

With all the energy that a south-eastern atmosphere can bring to the brain, it risks leading to being overly analytical when it might be better simply to get on with the task and learn, adapt and evolve as part of the process.

sensitive

Some people may feel more exposed and sensitive in this atmosphere, as they open up and lose their natural protection. It is possible to feel more hurt by criticism than is necessary, and to let someone else's bad mood affect your own emotions too deeply.

the psychological energy of the south

Have another look at the basic qualities of the energy of the south (see page 53). In order to experience this energy, go outside in the morning in June in the northern hemisphere (December in the southern hemisphere).

southern energy characteristics

- Fiery

- Passionate

- Emotional

- Expressive

- Sociable

- Quick-minded

- Warm

- Noticeable

- Stressed

- Argumentative

- Agitated

understanding southern energy

Here are some of the emotions that this energy brings with it. Be aware of the occasions on which you exhibit the characteristics below, so that you get to know the fire energy within.

fiery
The energy of the south has an outward, fiery quality that helps energy spread out through your body. This can result in feeling warm at your skin, and as if your blood is flowing to the tips of your fingers and toes.

passionate
Surges of hot, summer energy make the energy of the south ideal for experiencing rushes of passion. This can feel like strong sensations of love emanating from your heart.

emotional
The midday, sunny energy of the south helps emotions rise to the head, making you feel more aware of your feelings. This can lead to making decisions based on your emotions and mood at the time.

expressive
As the energy of the south moves quickly, it helps bring your emotions to the surface and express them. When southern energy is strong, other people will find it easy to read your mood.

sociable
The summery, outward atmosphere makes it easy to feel sociable. This can help you feel more like making friends and more outgoing when you are in company. By being more expressive, it becomes simpler to attract people into your social circle.

quick-minded
Fiery energy is fast and responsive, making this southern, summer energy

ideal for being quick-witted. A rush of fire energy to your head helps stimulate your mind and fill your head with ideas.

warm

Someone who is full of this energy will tend to feel warm-hearted and have a generous spirit. This can help you be more of a 'people person' and make strong emotional bonds with friends.

noticeable

Having an abundance of summer energy helps you shine and be noticeable. This can make you stand out in a crowd and make a memorable impression at social events or in your work.

stressed

Too much fiery energy risks leaving you feeling stressed and overwhelmed. At times your emotions may feel out of control and you may find it harder to step back and consider a problem rationally.

argumentative

An excess of summer energy can precipitate a quickness to react to perceived insults and misplaced pride. This often leads to unnecessary arguments and falling out with friends.

agitated

Fire energy is not relaxing, so, if you are of a nervous disposition, too much summer energy can make you ill at ease and generally agitated.

southern energy goals

Examples of goals to work with southern energy include:

- To attend dancing classes each week

- To join a debating club or discussion group and interact weekly

- To go out for a meal with your family or close friends each week

- To invite people to your home for dinner or a party each month

Left: Fiery energy can help enhance the expressive characteristics we use in social situations.

the psychological energy
of the south-west

Review the basic qualities of the energy of the south-west (see page 53). To experience this energy, go outside in the afternoon in July and August in the northern hemisphere (January and February in the southern hemisphere).

south-western energy characteristics

- Settled

- Down-to-earth

- Secure

- Practical

- Adding quality to life

- Cosy

- Slow

- Dull

understanding south-western energy

Here is a list of feelings that this energy can help to boost. As you read the characteristics of south-western energy, see if you can identify the things that you do and the emotions you experience that help you to feel this energy.

Right: Being on the floor and looking after a child can both enhance the south-western energy inside you.

settled

This summer-turning-to-autumn energy brings a more soothing atmosphere that helps you feel able to settle in one place and feel at home. It is an energy that leads you to focus more attention on your home and put more effort into creating the ideal nest to come back to.

down-to-earth

South-western energy moves your energy downward and helps you feel more connected to the earth. This creates the experience of being better grounded and having your feet firmly on the land.

secure

The downward, slower nature of this energy can help you feel more secure and stable. As the energy moves down to your abdomen, you can experience a warmth that induces sensations of security and nourishment.

practical

Moving energy down from the head to your physical body helps you focus on the more practical, functional aspects of life. This is an excellent energy to enable you to work methodically through a list of tasks and to function well in the real world.

adding quality to life

The summer-to-autumn quality of this energy carries the imagery of the fruit ripening on the vine. There is no further growth, but nature is taking what is there and making it sweeter, adding more quality. South-western energy is therefore ideal for making the most of what you have in life and for improving the quality of any aspect of your life.

cosy

The settling afternoon energy as the sun starts to go down in the sky helps you feel more cosy, comfortable and relaxed. It is good to bring this atmosphere into your home when you want to switch off from work and switch on to being close to your family and friends.

slow

South-western energy marks the beginning of the sun's waning phase, in terms of the day and the season, so too much can slow your energy and place too much focus on simply working with what you have. In extremes it could make someone cautious about taking on anything new.

dull

Too much downward-moving south-western energy can move energy away from your head, leaving you with less energy for new ideas, inspiration and the intellectual enthusiasm to explore new subjects.

south-western energy goals

Examples of goals to work with south-western energy include:

- To spend at least one hour a day playing with your children

- To make a point of spending half a day each week with someone close to you and giving them your full attention

- To make an improvement to your home each month

- To do one sympathetic, charitable or helpful act each month

the psychological energy of the west

Remember the basic qualities of the energy of the west (see page 53). To experience this energy, go out and watch the sunset in September in the northern hemisphere (March in the southern hemisphere).

western energy characteristics

- Complete
- Satisfied
- Joyous
- Pleased
- Reflective
- Romantic
- Having inner strength
- Depressed
- Withdrawn
- Inward-looking

understanding western energy

Here are suggestions concerning the emotions that this energy can enhance. Use these descriptions to sense when you have the most western energy.

complete

The sunset, autumn energy signifies the end of the day and harvest time, making a western energy ideal for feeling better able to fulfil projects or tasks. In general this can lead to stronger sensations of feeling complete about life.

satisfied

The western energy associated with the end to the working day can increase feelings of satisfaction and contentment. You might find this a helpful energy to come home to when you want to relax after a day's work.

joyous

The end-of-the-day feeling and time of the harvest are associated with joy in classical Chinese thinking. This is a happy time filled with sensations of satisfaction, completion and accomplishment, as well as moving into a time of rest.

pleased

As the sunset could, for many people, mark the change from work to relaxation and enjoyment, western energy is associated with the pleasures of life and with taking life less seriously.

reflective

The symbol of the lake and mirror-like surface brings in the association of self-reflection. Sitting watching the sun set at the end of the day can be a helpful environment in which to reflect on what has happened, what was done and how it might have been done better or differently.

romantic

The playful nature of the sunset energy is associated with romance. It is when many would consider going out on a romantic date, and for some watching the sun slowly set is a romantic experience in itself.

having inner strength

The inward movement of this energy helps bring in and keep energy deep inside you. This is ideal when you want to develop greater inner strength. You might use this to develop your willpower and tenacity.

depressed

Too much inward-flowing energy can lead to feelings of self-absorption, depression and the inability to reach out for help. This might be particularly acute if your energy is moving slowly and is already thin.

withdrawn

Strong inward-moving energy risks you being withdrawn and only making minimal contact with people, if the inward energy is too strong for the upward and outward energies and overwhelms them, it reduces their influence on the body.

inward-looking

When there is an excess of western energy, you may become overly concerned with your own pleasures and, in terms of work or other pursuits, appear lazy and uninterested.

western energy goals

Examples of goals to work with west energy include:

- To do something romantic with your lover each week

- To give someone flowers each month

- To write a romantic poem, card or letter to someone close to you each month

- To complete one overdue project each month

Romance and joy are fundamental characteristics of western energy.

the psychological energy of the north-west

Review the basic qualities of the energy of the north-western (see page 53). To experience this energy, go out in the evening in October and November in the northern hemisphere (April and May in the southern hemisphere).

north-western energy characteristics

- Dignified
- Prepared
- Responsible
- Wise
- Organized
- Showing leadership
- Showing integrity
- Judgemental
- Unrealistic standards

understanding north-western energy

Below are my suggestions concerning the emotions that this energy can bring. See if any of these resonate strongly with you to access the north-western energy inside.

dignified
The symbolism of heaven coupled with the end-of-the-cycle energy of the evening and the latter part of the year can produce an energetic quality of dignity, where everything has been experienced before and someone knows from experience what to do. This is an energy that can help you command respect and be taken seriously.

prepared
In terms of traditional agriculture, this is seen as a time of preservation, storing, drying and pickling, so that there is food for the winter. For this reason north-western energy is associated with readying yourself before beginning events. It is an ideal energy for feeling better prepared and able to organize yourself as well as others.

responsible
As north-western energy comes at the end of the seasonal and daily cycle, it is seen as the most mature energy, making it one that is suited to taking on responsibilities.

wise
Being associated with the heavens gives north-western energy a connection with wisdom. For this reason it is often also linked to intuition and being a mentor and helping others.

organized
This inward, end-of-the-cycle energy is ideal for feeling better organized and planning ahead for the next cycle: planning for tomorrow or next year and being better prepared for it.

Left: Having the life experience and wisdom to help others describes north-western energy.

showing leadership

The more serious, experienced, mature aspect of this energy makes it helpful when you want to take on a leadership position. With more north-western energy, others may take you more seriously and feel that you have the qualities to win the respect of others.

showing integrity

The symbol of heaven helps someone with more north-western energy do things with integrity and honesty. This helps you be more forthright and put a greater emphasis on telling the truth.

judgemental

People with an abundance of north-western energy like to feel in control and able to organize themselves. Sometimes this can spill over into organizing others in a way that is not healthy for either person.

unrealistic standards

With an excess of energy associated with the heavens, it is possible to set unrealistic standards for yourself and those around you. This can not only lead to disappointment, but may risk you appearing judgemental, belittling and condescending to others.

north-western energy goals

Examples of goals to work with north-western energy include:

- To plan out and organize each month at the beginning of the month

- To listen to and act on your intuition once a month

- To take on the role of being a mentor to someone each year

- To make a list each evening of things to do the following day

feng shui
life-coaching tools

You will now learn about the practical tools you need in order to apply feng shui life coaching in your home. You will first learn how to link your energies to feng shui tools (see pages 76–79). You will then discover how to map your home according to the energies of the eight directions (see pages 80–89), as well as how to use tools such as colour (see pages 90–91), materials (see pages 92–93), lighting (see pages 94–95) and other decorating tools (see pages 96–113) to bring about your life goals. You can then use these tools immediately to change the way you feel in a room. In addition, you will find out how to make the most of the seasons, lunar cycles, equinoxes and solstices (see pages 114–119).

inner energetic change

You can link your own energies — and your desired energies — with feng shui tools. To a certain extent this is an individual matter: you will have to discover for yourself what particular energy flow within you makes it easier to transform your emotions and set about achieving your personal goals. However, as all human beings have a lot in common, I will generalize here to get you started. As you begin to feel more confident about the process, you can experience for yourself the connection between certain atmospheres and emotions.

Below: Be aware of the energy flow that accompanies each of your moods.

your home and your emotions

As already discussed (see pages 48–49), we can describe the energy of a home and of humans in terms of its direction, speed, density and volatility. The idea is that if slow, outward, thin, consistent energy helps you feel peaceful, then placing yourself in room with the same atmosphere will make it easier for you to feel tranquil.

Each time you experience a strong emotion, think about how your energy is moving. For example, when you are angry, you might feel that your energy is moving out rapidly, is concentrated and volatile. When you feel depressed, you might sense that your energy is moving in an inward, slow, concentrated and consistent way. In this manner you can connect your emotions with energy.

changing your energy

You can also think in terms of the energy of each of the eight directions. In the charts that follow I have made suggestions concerning which energy most closely describes each emotional state. But some emotions can be a combination of different kinds of energy, so rather than referring just to 'northern energy' you might talk in terms of 'northern energy with more of this-or-that energy'.

Use the charts to see how to change your energy; then use your knowledge of feng shui to see how you can alter the energy of your home and bring in more of the kind of energy you need. I have suggested some items that might help, including colours, materials, lighting, shapes, plants, water features, sea salt, clocks, wind chimes, bells and mirrors. These tools are dicussed further later on in the chapter.

unhelpful energies

These are emotions that are not particularly helpful to you. If you identify an emotion or state of mind that applies to you, note the type of energy flow, then use the advice given below and elsewhere in this book to bring in the *opposite* energies.

Emotion or state of mind	Energy flow and direction	Helped by its opposite
Anger	Up and out, fast, concentrated, volatile; east	Beige, brown, grey, pink; fabrics, carpets; table or floor lamps; curves; ivy, money plant; pond; west
Depression	Inward, slow, concentrated, consistent; north-west	Cream, orange, purple, red, yellow; glass; peace lily; aquarium, fountain; wind chimes; bells; mirrors; crystals; south
Anxiety	Multi-directional, fast, thin, volatile; south	Grey; carpets; clocks; south-west and north-west
Fear	Inward, fast, concentrated, volatile; north	Orange, yellow; carpets; cyclamen, money plant; east and south-east
Panic or hysteria	Outward, fast, concentrated, volatile; south	Beige, black, brown, grey; carpets; curves; ivy, money plant; pond; sea salt; clocks; north
Unrealistic expectations	Up, fast, concentrated, consistent; east	Cream; curves; ivy; aquarium; north
Jealousy	Down, slow, concentrated, volatile; south-west	Blue, green, turquoise; wood; hyacinth, peace lily; fountain; south-east
Excessive criticism	Inward, slow, concentrated, consistent; north-east	Cream, orange, pink, purple; ivy, peace lily; fountain; wind chimes; bells; convex mirrors; crystals; north
Shyness	Inward, slow, thin, consistent; west	Orange, purple, red, yellow; polished wooden floor; lights; fountain; south
Unhelpful assumptions	Inward, fast, concentrated, consistent; north-west	Cream, yellow; candles; curves; cyclamen; bells; north

helpful energies in certain situations

These are typical emotions or states of mind that you might want to experience more often. If one of them appeals to you, use the information given in the following pages to bring more of the *same* energy into your home.

Emotion or state of mind	Energy flow and direction	Helped by
Assertiveness, confidence	Up, fast, concentrated, consistent; east	Green, blue, turquoise; shiny stone floor, polished wooden floor; dracaena
Expressiveness	Up and out, fast, concentrated, fluid; south	Purple, red; shiny stone floor, polished wooden floor; uplighters; dracaena; fountain
Feeling in control	Inward, slow, concentrated, consistent; north-west	Black, grey, maroon; sea salt
Letting go	Outward, steady, thin, fluid; north-east	White; candles; peace lily; wind chimes; convex mirrors; crystals
A more flexible perspective on life	Multi-directional, steady, even, fluid; north	Cream, yellow, white; curves; ivy; mirrors; water
Inner strength	Inward, steady, concentrated, consistent; north-west	Black, grey; sea salt
Practicality	Down, steady, even, consistent; south-west	Beige, brown; fabrics; waterfall
Objectivity	Multi-directional, slow, thin, fluid; north	Cream; curves; ivy, money plant; water
Creativity	Up and out, fast, even, fluid; south-east	Green, purple, turquoise; shiny stone floor, polished wooden floor; lights; dracaena, peace lily; fountain; wind chimes; convex mirrors
Imagination	Up and out, steady, thin, fluid; south-east and north	Blue, turquoise, yellow; wood; cyclamen, hyacinth, peace lily; clocks; wind chimes; crystals
Passion	Out, fast, concentrated, volatile; south	Orange, purple, red; lights; bells
Sympathy	Down and inward, slow, even, consistent; south-west	Beige, brown, grey; fabrics, carpets; table or floor lamps; sea salt

Emotion or state of mind	Energy flow and direction	Helped by
Motherliness, security, cosiness	Down, slow, even, consistent; south-west	Beige, brown; fabrics, carpets; table or floor lamps
Contentedness	Inward, steady, even, fluid; west	Pink, rusty red, light grey; soft stone; floor lamps

Below: Lie down in a tranquil environment and carefully listen to your body. Practise feeling how your energy moves. Are you more aware of your head, heart, stomach or abdomen?

creating an eight-direction
house map

On the following pages you will discover how to read the natural flow of eight-direction energy through your home. This is an important principle in feng shui and gives you a basic map that lets you read the atmosphere of your home and get ideas about how it might influence you.

energy and your house

When considering the natural energy and atmosphere in your home, you can use the movement of the sun as the main influence. Every day your home experiences the cycle of the sun moving around it, energizing it with its solar energy. So a pattern of energy flow becomes established over the years, according to the relationship between the sun and your living space. Although this energy can be affected by the interior design of your home and by the people living there, the eight directions provide the basic energetic plan for your home.

eight-direction example

For example, you can assume that the south side (north in the southern hemisphere) will have the hot, sunny, bright atmosphere that is associated with the feeling of midday and summer. In contrast, the north side (south in the southern hemisphere) of your home will feel comparatively colder, darker and stiller — more like the atmosphere experienced in the night and winter.

You can then work from the centre of your home in each direction, matching it up with the kind of atmosphere you can experience there by linking the direction with its appropriate time of day and season. In nature this is a gradual progression as the sun slowly rises in the sky in the east and moves through to setting in the west. However, to make life easier, you can think of eight distinct energies: essentially the four cardinal directions (north, east, south and west) and the four directions in between (north-east, south-east, south-west and north-west).

To help understand the energy flow in your home it is beneficial to know where these eight directions lie. Once you have established this, you will know which part of your home lies, for example, to the east and therefore which area is likely to have a rising, sunrise, springtime atmosphere.

using the map

Photocopy the eight direction map on page 82 for a quick reference for any home or work space, without having to draw the eight directions on each floor plan. You can then read the notes about each direction on the acetate or transparency while still seeing the floor plan underneath.

Left: An eight-direction house map is an excellent quick guide to accompany any house plan.

the eight-direction house map

On this map the cardinal points (north, south, east and west) occupy 30 degrees each; the in-between directions take up 60-degree segments. The chart is written for use in the northern hemisphere, so you will need to alter the directions as previously stated (see pages 50–53) if you are using it for a home in the southern hemisphere.

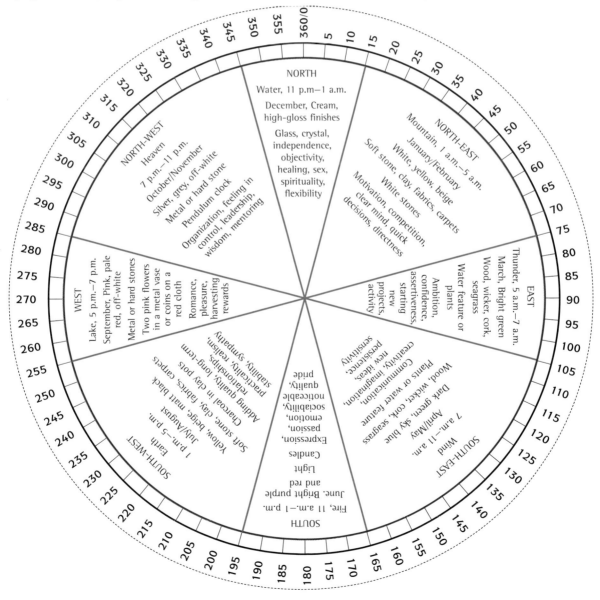

using the map

Opposite is a map of the eight directions. You can photocopy this onto a transparency (a sheet of acetate/transparent film) for laying over your floor plans and instantly seeing where each of the eight directions in your home lies. The map can then be used as a quick reference concerning the qualities of each direction.

Once you have made a copy, cut around the outer dotted line to make the transparency easier to use. The numbers on the outside will be used to align the transparency with a compass reading (see page 87).

You can then either simply place the centre of the transparency over what you think is the centre of the floor plan, or you can use the method described on page 86 to find out more accurately where the centre of your floor plan is.

If you know where the midday sun is from your home, then you can simply turn your transparency so that its southern segment is facing that direction. You may find this easier if the floor plan itself is at the correct orientation.

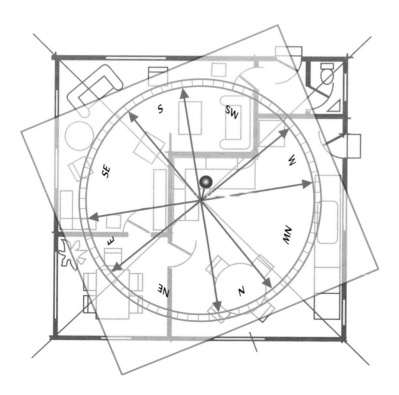

what the eight-direction map reveals

For each area the map shows you:

- The relevant direction

- The symbol from nature

- The relevant time of day

- The associated months of the year

- The colours that represent the energy of that direction

- The materials that encourage the flow of energy linked with that direction

- A special item that could boost the energy connected with that direction

- The human emotions, behaviour and mental state that can be enhanced by the energy of that direction

watching the sun

The traditional method of working out how the eight directions are orientated in your home is to observe the sun. This will tell you in which direction north, east, south and west lie in your home and will enable you to be aware of how the sun enters it throughout the day. Observe the movement of the sun for a few days and look for the sun's direction at its highest point in the sky, at midday. This will be to the south in the northern hemisphere and to the north in the southern hemisphere.

use the sun's shadow

If you have a garden, you can push a long stick into the ground and watch the shadow move through the day. As the sun rises in the morning, the shadow will point in a westerly direction. When the sun reaches its highest point at midday, the shadow will point north in the northern hemisphere and south in the southern hemisphere. As the sun sets, the shadow will point in an easterly direction. You can peg out a sheet of paper, pierce the stick through the centre and then draw out the shadow on the paper and write down the time every hour, to establish how the sun moves around your garden (and your home) throughout the day. If you do not have a garden, simply note the position of the sun in the sky at different times throughout the day, to work out how it moves around your home.

You can use this information to assess which parts of your home face to the north, east, south and west. You can then orientate your transparency of the eight directions (see pages 82–83). Once you know the direction of south, stand in the central part of your home and hold your transparency so that south on it faces in the same direction as the midday sun. Now you will be able to see where all the other directions lie in your home.

the sun and your home

Using this method can give you a better real-life, intuitive understanding of the relationship between the sun and your home. For example, see where the eastern sun enters your home between the hours of 5 a.m. and 7 a.m. and which parts of your home it touches with its rising solar energy. You can then get to know where the sun comes into your home in each of its eight phases. As you become familiar with the times of the day and the position of the sun, you will realize where each of the eight directions of energy are in your home. You will now have a guide to which kind of energy you can generally expect to find in different parts of your home, according to the environmental influence of the sun.

Left: A pole will cast a shadow showing the position of the sun. Remember that the shadow points in the opposite direction.

sun times

This chart shows the position of the sun at different times of the day. Note that the closer you live to the north or south pole, the earlier the sun will rise in the summer and the later in the winter. The directions for the southern hemisphere are given in brackets.

Direction	Times
North (South)	11 p.m.—1 a.m.
North-east (South-east)	1 a.m.—5 a.m.
East	5 a.m.—7 a.m.
South-east (North-east)	7 a.m.—11 a.m.
South (North)	11 a.m.—1 p.m.
South-west (North-west)	1 p.m.—5 p.m.
West	5 p.m.—7 p.m.
North-west (South-west)	7 p.m.—11 p.m.

applying the eight-direction house map

If you have floor plans of your home, you can lay the eight-direction transparency over them. To do so you will need to know approximately where the centre of your home is, take a compass reading, then orientate the transparency correctly over the plan. If you don't have any floor plans, you can either get some drawn up or sketch them yourself.

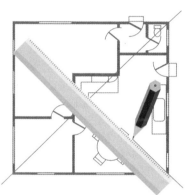

Above: The point at which two diagonal lines from the corners cross marks the centre.

finding the centre of your house

To apply the transparency, you need to know where the centre of your home is on your floor plan.

• If your home is rectangular (or almost rectangular), draw a rectangle that most closely matches the perimeter of your home. Then draw diagonal lines between the corners: the point at which they cross is the centre. (If you live in an apartment, only include the areas that are for your sole use – not any shared areas.)

• If your home is an unusual shape, such as an L-shape, divide it into two rectangles and find the centre of each rectangle, as described above. Then draw a dotted line between the two centres. Do the same again, but this time dividing the home into the other two possible rectangles. The point where the dotted lines cross is the centre.

• If your home is a complicated shape and you like to play with geometry, divide your home into different rectangles and draw diagonal lines to find the centre of each one. Then draw lines between the various centres. The centre point of two rectangles will be on a line. Measure the length of each line. Measure the sides of each rectangle and multiply the length and width of each rectangle to find its area. Now you can take two adjoining rectangles and apply the following formula:

The centre point along the line = the total length of the line divided by the area of the two rectangles and then multiplied by the area of the smallest rectangle.

Use the answer to measure along the line from the centre of the larger rectangle to find the centre of the two rectangles combined. Now you can draw a line from this new centre to the centre of the next rectangle and apply the same formula.

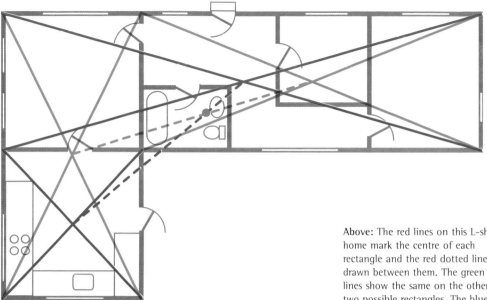

Above: The red lines on this L-shaped home mark the centre of each rectangle and the red dotted line is drawn between them. The green lines show the same on the other two possible rectangles. The blue dot marks the point where they cross and the centre of the L-shape.

using a compass

It is essential to use a compass if you cannot see the sun from your home or the weather is too cloudy to see it.

Stand inside your home and point the body of your compass towards the front wall. Walk around your home to find a satisfactory place to do this, because magnetic items (such as electrical equipment, radiators, girders and pipes in walls) can give you a false reading. When you are happy with the reading, turn the dial and make a note of the degrees, while keeping the compass body facing the front wall. If you are unsure of your reading, you can check it using a street map. There will be a slight discrepancy because magnetic north is a few degrees different from the polar north on maps.

aligning the eight directions

Next, draw a line on your floor plan from the centre of your home straight through the front of your home.

Put your eight-directions transparency over your floor plan so that its middle lies over the centre mark on your floor plan. Turn the transparency so that the compass reading you took when facing the front of your home is the same as the reading on the transparency where it meets the line drawn from the centre to the front of your home. Now you will be able to see where each of the eight directions lies in your home.

Below: Point the body of the compass at the front wall and turn the outer ring so that north lines up with the pointed end of the needle. This gives you a reading.

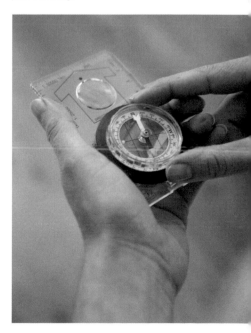

assessing the eight-direction house map

The shape of your floor plan and the position of your windows and doors will show you which of the eight types of energy is predominant in your home and is likely to have the greatest influence on you. If the area of your floor plan is similar under the different directions, then your home contains a good balance of the eight energies, making it easier to lead a well-balanced life.

Right: Skylights bring sunlight, increasing the vertical flow of energy, and helping a room feel taller.

Remember that in this system the cardinal points (north, east, south and west) occupy 30 degrees each, while the in-between directions take up 60-degree segments, so it is normal for south-east to take up twice the area of east. A square home will contain almost-even segments. Long narrow homes, L-shaped footprints and complicated shapes will result in some directions covering large areas of the home, while other directions cover a smaller space or none at all.

missing energies

If any of the energies are deficient, make a note of them and consult your transparency or the more comprehensive description on pages 58–73 to see if this is affecting your life. For example, if there is no east on your floor plan, you might lack confidence, self-esteem and ambition, as well as find it harder to start new projects.

You can boost the missing energy using the suggestions shown for that direction on your transparency. Sometimes you will have to put the cures outside your home, if the direction in question is missing altogether. When there is no correlation between the deficient energy and your real life, you may find that the energy has been compensated for by some other means, such as the windows and doors.

points of energy access

Most environmental energy will enter your home through the doors and windows, although some can enter through the floor, roof and walls. Skylights greatly increase this flow, creating wider exposure to the mentally and spiritually stimulating energy from the sky. This increases the vertical flow of energy, and this will help you to feel more intellectually independent.

The location of your doors and windows from the centre will define which kind of energy more readily enters your home. The larger the door or window, the more energy will flow through it; the more people who use the door, the more energy will be encouraged to come through it. Full, heavy curtains (even when drawn back) slow down the flow of energy through a window.

Look up on your transparency the kind of energy a door or window in that position brings in. If you have a choice of entrances, decide which one promotes the kind of energy that would best help you in your life, then use that door more often. See if any of the windows face a direction that will bring in more of the energy you think you need, then make sure this window is kept uncovered as much as possible and open it daily.

Above: Big windows bring in energy but also increase the horizontal flow of energy, helping a room feel wider.

colours

The colours in your home represent a powerful influence on your mood and the atmosphere of your home. Large surfaces such as walls, floors and ceilings have the greatest influence, but even relatively small areas of colour – perhaps in a vase of flowers, a cushion or a blind – can make a strong contribution to a room's energy. The general rule is: the brighter the colour, the greater the influence (even if it only covers a relatively small area).

Below: A strong pattern of colours can create a stimulating environment, but not one for relaxing.

colours and the eight directions

You can think of different colours in terms of the eight directions of energy and the way in which a certain hue might directly change the energy in your home. Again, the brighter the colour, the stronger the effect. So if you wanted to feel more tranquil and you decided that more northern energy would help, you would paint your room cream. In the list below, the directions for the southern hemisphere are given in brackets.

- North (South) Cream, pink, white, silver, grey, glossy black
- North-east (South-east) White, yellow, purple
- East Green, turquoise
- South-east (North-east) Green, blue, turquoise
- South (North) Green, blue, purple, red
- South-west (North-west) Beige, brown, orange, matt black
- West Maroon, pink, yellow, white
- North-west (South-west) White, grey, silver, yellow

colour and energy

You can also look at colours in terms of the way they influence the movement of energy in your home. Remind yourself of the energy descriptions given on page 49 in relation to direction, speed, density and volatility.

Look at the description of how you want to change your energy on pages 76–77 and see which of the colours opposite most closely matches the kind of energy you felt would be most helpful. For example, if being more expressive meant making your energy move up and out, faster, in a more concentrated and fluid way, then more red might help because it has the same characteristics. In the descriptions opposite there is also a line on each colour's link to nature.

colour, movement and nature

Colour	Energy flow	Link to nature
Beige	Down, slow, even, consistent	Burnt grasses in summer, sun-kissed earth, wild grains
Black	Inward, slow, concentrated, consistent	Darkest night, a long cave, rich earth, deep water, shade
Blue	Up, steady, thin, fluid	Bright, clear sky, the sea on a sunny day, wild flowers
Brown	Down, slow, even, consistent	Summer changing to autumn, fading, falling leaves, bare earth
Cream	Multi-directional, steady, thin, fluid	Clouds, foam from surf, fast-running river, the moon
Green	Up, fast, even, fluid	Spring, new shoots, grasses, trees, plants
Grey	Inward, slow, even, consistent	Heavy clouds, cold water, stone, rocks, high mountains
Maroon	Inward, steady, concentrated, volatile	Sunset, roses, rocks, thistles, wild flowers, autumn leaves
Orange	Outward, fast, concentrated, volatile	The sun
Pink	Inward, steady, thin, fluid	Sunset, wild flowers, rocks
Purple	Outward, fast, even, volatile	Hot summer haze, wild flowers, thistles
Red	Outward, fast, concentrated, fluid	Wild flowers
Turquoise	Up, steady, thin, fluid	The sea, spring changing to summer
Yellow	Outward, steady, even, fluid	Corn, sunflowers, wild flowers, butterflies, bees
White	Multi-directional, fast, thin, fluid	Stars, snow-capped mountains, frost, crystals, stones, chalk

materials

The materials used in your home — whether stone floor, wooden furniture or linen curtains — alter the way in which energy flows through a room. As a generalization, the harder, shinier and flatter the surface, the faster energy flows across it, speeding up the general energy flow throughout a room. A typical example would be a polished marble floor. Conversely soft, matt, textured surfaces, such a rug, slow down the energy in a room.

materials and the eight directions

You can also associate the different materials used in a home with each of the eight directions of energy. This can help you bring into a room more of the particular energy that you have identified as generating successful emotions within you.

Below: A shiny floor in a tall room reflects energy, creating a strong upward flow.

To make the effect stronger, you can use certain materials in the appropriate directions — for example, a wooden floor in the east — although this does not mean that you have to do this; you could use wood in any part of your home if you wanted to create a more eastern, upward, sunrise, springtime atmosphere there. In this list the directions for the southern hemisphere are given in brackets.

- North (South) Hard stone, glass, metal
- North-east (South-east) Hard stone
- East Wood
- South-east (North-east) Wood
- South (North) Polished wood
- South-west (North-west) Plaster, fabrics
- West Hard stone, metal
- North-west (South-west) Matt stone, metal

So a room with a wooden floor, wooden blinds and wooden furniture might have a morning, springtime, eastern feel, whereas a room with a stone floor, metal furniture and glass surfaces might have a more sunset, autumnal, western atmosphere. Rugs or a carpet, soft furnishings, curtains and tapestries will give more of a summer-autumn, south-western feel.

materials and energy

In addition, you can think of each type of surface in terms of the way it can change the energy in a room, using this information to link back to pages 76–77 where you explored which kind of energy would help you most.

So if you wanted to feel more creative, previously you would have considered an atmosphere that was up and out, fast, even and fluid. Now a room that has a polished hardwood floor (up, fast, concentrated, fluid), bare wooden furniture (up, steady, dispersed, consistent) and plaster walls (outward, steady, dispersed, fluid) would help you. Likewise, to feel caring, secure and cosy, you would be helped by energy that moves downward, slowly, evenly and consistently, so living in a room with woollen carpets or rugs, linen curtains and big cotton cushions would be advantageous.

materials and energy flow

Materials	Energy flow
Bare wooden blinds, floor and furniture	Up, steady, thin, consistent
Cotton cushions and upholstery	Down, slow, even, consistent
Hard, shiny stone floors	Up, fast, concentrated, fluid
Glass table-tops and mirrors	Multi-directional, fast, even, fluid
Linen curtains	Down, slow, concentrated, consistent
Metal furniture	Inward, fast, concentrated, fluid
Plaster walls	Outward, steady, thin, fluid
Polished hardwood floors	Up, fast, concentrated, fluid
Polished hardwood furniture	Multi-directional, fast, concentrated, fluid
Shiny wallpaper or paint	Inward, fast, concentrated, fluid
Soft, textured stone floors	Multi-directional, steady, thin, fluid
Woollen carpets and soft furnishings	Down, slow, even, consistent

candles and lights

Candles and lights are a quick and effective way to change the atmosphere in a room. At the strike of a match or the flick of a switch you can alter the lighting in the evening and, as a result, transform your mood. Lights and candles are generally associated with the fire energy of the south and their use will increase the presence of this midday, sunny energy in your home.

experiment with lighting

To get new ideas for lighting, take a powerful torch or a light on a lead into a dark room and shine the beam in different ways to see how various forms of lighting will affect the room. Use a card to help shade the light in differing ways. Pay attention to the mood that certain lighting effects have, and how this influences your emotions. When you find an effect that you like, buy the appropriate lighting.

In addition you can use a bright lamp and hold pieces of coloured transparency/film over the light to establish the effect of having different kinds of coloured lighting in a particular room. Also experiment with holding some thin paper or fabric safely in front of the lamp, to experience the effect of shading and diffused light.

There are many different kinds of lighting – we will examine each one in terms of the way it influences the energy of a room.

Below: These light boxes diffuse and soften the light spreading it in every direction.

lighting and energy

Type of lighting	Energy flow	Characteristics
Candles	Outward, slow, thin, volatile	Candles produce a warm orange light and have the unique feature of flickering, which brings a moving light with changing intensity; the shadows in a candlelit room move slightly, creating a blurred, soft effect
Ceiling lights	Outward, fast, concentrated, fluid	Sitting in a room with a single light source has a more natural feel, since there are only single shadows, rather than the multi-directional shadows created by several competing light sources
Spotlights and halogen lights	Outward, fast, concentrated, fluid	These produce an intense white light focused strongly on one point; such light tends to be stimulating and can highlight interesting features in a room
Table lamps, salt lamps and lampshades	Down, slow, thin, consistent	Table lamps and salt lamps (hollowed-out blocks of salt with a bulb inside) create a cosy atmosphere, while lampshades make the light feel softer: a coarse paper shade with specks of dense material will form a speckled shadow on the walls; to bring the energy further down, site the lamp on the floor
Uplighters	Up, fast, concentrated, fluid	Uplighters shine onto a ceiling, making it appear brighter than the floor (as in nature, where the sky is brighter than the ground); try positioning a free-standing uplighter in a corner to provide an interesting light source
Wall lamps	Up, steady, thin, fluid	Wall lamps that reflect light onto the wall and then into the room can provide an interesting diffused effect, where soft light emerges from various parts of the room, with gentle gradations in intensity

shapes

The shapes and forms within a home or room further alter the way in which energy moves. Because these features are not easy to transform, you can employ other energy-changing tools to compensate for a fixed feature that is, for instance, moving energy too quickly. For example, you might position a series of houseplants along a long corridor to break up long, straight lines of energy.

shapes and energy

Shape	Energy flow	Characteristics
Curves	Multi-directional, slow, even, fluid	Curved walls change the direction of energy and tend to slow it down; curved furniture enables energy to move smoothly through a room, making a space feel more harmonious and less turbulent so that it may be perceived as being more relaxing
Horizontal lines	Horizontal, steady, concentrated, fluid	Horizontal lines in the form of picture rails, coving, windowsills, pelmets, long windows and furniture make a room feel broader, but lower; the atmosphere feels compressed and moving horizontally — useful when you want to feel better connected to other people
Internal corners	Inward, slow, even, consistent	With internal corners there is a risk that energy will get stuck and contribute to the room feeling stagnant; this is most likely to occur if the corners are cluttered and less likely if you grow plants in the corners or clean them regularly
Long corridors	Horizontal, fast, concentrated, volatile	Energy can move quickly along long, straight corridors, and the flow will be faster if the floors are polished and the walls smooth; this can impel people along, but is less helpful if the corridor leads straight into a bedroom where you want to relax

Right: The curve of this room encourages energy to flow smoothly across the wall's surface and will make the room feel more harmonious.

Shape	Energy flow	Characteristics
Long, straight surfaces	Multi-directional, fast, even, volatile	Long, straight surfaces encourage energy to speed up in a room, especially when the surfaces are hard and shiny; a square or rectangular room with little furniture or long, flat furniture will feel alive and vital, but may be harder to feel at peace in
Protruding corners and edges	Multi-directional, fast, concentrated, volatile	As energy moves across the protruding edge in an L-shaped room or across the angular edge of a cabinet or shelving, it can start to swirl and become turbulent, giving a stimulating (but chaotic) feel, where you may feel a bit disorientated
Vertical lines	Up and down, steady, even, fluid	Vertical stripes, columns, long curtains, tall windows, doors and furniture can create the impression that a room is taller; this can help you feel more independent, mentally stimulated and inspired, as the vertical ambient energy runs up through your head
Sloping ceilings	Outward, steady, concentrated, volatile	In a tall room, a sloping ceiling can bring in a more fiery, summer, midday energy, which can feel stimulating and inspirational; if the ceiling is low, the slope can compress the energy, creating a more confining feel

space

Different rooms contain their own distinct atmospheres, depending on their proportions and shape. The windows and doors in a room further influence the flow of energy. It would be hard to change the shape of a room, but the following information can help you choose the appropriate room in which to create the mood you require in order to succeed.

space and energy

Space	Energy flow	Characteristics
High ceilings	Up, steady, even, fluid	Under high ceilings the energy is free to move vertically, and leaves a great space about your head into which your own mental energy can expand; this can leave you feeling free and better able to think creatively, and you may also find it mentally stimulating
Low ceilings	Horizontal, steady, even, fluid	Under low ceilings the energy moves horizontally, making it easier to feel connected to other people and be practical as your energy mixes with theirs; this is ideal for team working and for creating harmony
Upper floors	Up and horizontal, fast, thin, volatile	The higher up in a building you are, the more you are exposed to the sun and sky; the surrounding energy will move freely in and out of your home, making it a potentially stimulating, inspiring place in which to live
Ground floors	Down and horizontal, steady, concentrated, fluid	The lower you are in a building (and in particular in basements and ground floors), the more you will be influenced by the energy of the earth across the land around you; this makes you feel closely connected to society and part of the local community

Left: This rooms has windows, glass doors and a skylight, encouraging energy to flow in and out freely.

Space	Energy flow	Characteristics
Many windows and large doors	Multi-directional, fast, even, volatile	A room with many large windows enables energy to move in and out freely, making for a refreshing space; you may feel your own mood change quickly, and such an atmosphere should help you feel more alive and ready for something new
Small windows and doors	Multi-directional, slow, thin, consistent	A room with small windows contains energy and reduces its flow into the room; the energy within will be more isolated if the walls are thick; you may feel still, quiet and sedentary — helpful when you feel like escaping into a dark cave to rest
Skylights	Up and down, fast, even, fluid	Skylights bring environmental energy through the ceiling, increasing the vertical flow of energy in a room; they can also give you a greater connection to the sky, sun, moon and stars, stimulating your imagination and creativity
Long, narrow rooms	Horizontal, fast, even, fluid	Long, narrow rooms and gallery spaces help energy flow along the room; if the windows are along one of the long walls, the energy will be predominantly from one direction, boosting certain emotions, depending on the direction the windows face

plants

All living things bring natural energy into your home, and one of the best ways to do this is with houseplants. Modern buildings can be deficient in terms of their internal energy and atmosphere, due to contemporary insulation materials and the extensive use of synthetics that often inhibit the flow of ambient environmental energy into a home, so having a variety of plants is ideal. In general plants are associated with the energy of the sunrise, spring and east.

using plants' energy

When choosing houseplants, it is vital to get ones that will thrive in the light, soil and air conditions in which you want to place them. Healthy, growing plants in your home are more important than any other considerations. You can, however, also think of plants in terms of the kind of energy they give out. The easiest way to do this is to look at the shape of the plant and see how the energy moves through it.

For example, a yucca moves energy strongly up and out through its pointed leaves. So you can say that its energy would be *up* and *out*; *fast* because the leaves are straight and strong; *concentrated* because the ends of the leaves are sharp and pointed; and *fluid* because the energy moves easily.

Grow plants with pointed leaves in corners to help stimulate potentially stagnant energy. Place bushy plants in front of protruding corners to calm and slow the fast, swirling energy generated by the sharp edge. Grow as many plants as possible in your bathroom because they soak up any excess dampness.

Left: Plants such as these help to move energy up and out. Their big, open leaves help to spread energy.

plants and energy

Plant	Energy flow	Characteristics
Cyclamen (*Cyclamen persicum*)	Up and horizontal, slow, even, fluid	The flowers send energy up, while the leaves move energy out horizontally; the broad leaves slow the flow of energy and the delicate petals generate an even, fluid energy
Dracaena (*Dracaena marginata*)	Up, fast, concentrated, fluid	The long, straight, pointed leaves send energy up quickly, concentrating it at the ends and moving the energy fluidly
Hyacinth (*Hyacinthus orientalis*)	Up, steady, thin, fluid	The leaves and flowers move energy straight up, although the flowers are more delicate and intricate, creating a thinner, more fluid flow
Ivy (*Hedera helix*)	Multi-directional, steady, thin, fluid	This plant spreads energy in all directions, stirring up the atmosphere with its many multi-pointed leaves
Money plant (*Crassula ovata*)	Multi-directional, slow, thin, consistent	The round leaves let out energy slowly and gently; because they grow in many directions, the energy moves out evenly.
Peace lily (*Spathiphyllum wallisii*)	Up and out, steady, even, fluid	The leaves grow up and out and end in distinct points; the peace lily's many leaves make this a vibrant plant
Poinsettia (*Euphorbia pulcherrima*)	Down and horizontal, slow, thin, consistent	The floppy leaves hang down, with soft red bracts sitting on top; this feeds energy low down in a room
Spider plant (*Chlorophytum comosum*)	Multi-directional, steady, even, fluid	Although the long, straight, pointed leaves start by growing up, they then tumble down in many directions, spreading energy quickly at all points

water

The human body is essentially made of water, and the energy of the water inside your body has a similar energetic frequency to any water nearby, making it possible to create a powerful connection between the two. If the energy of the water outside your body is pure and clear, it can help improve the quality of the energy of the water inside your body. People have traditionally gone to the sea, spas or springs to heal and recover from illness. This practice gives credence to the feng shui principle of immersing yourself in the energy of fresh, clean water for its restorative, healing influence.

water features in the home

You can add more of this water energy to your home and garden. Not only may it help you feel more healthy, but a water feature inside a room or an enclosed part of a garden will change the atmosphere. In addition, a moving water feature has the practical advantage of producing a multi-frequency white sound that can mute some of the frequencies of other, unwanted noises. A large fountain will also clean dust from the air and charge it with more positive ions (which are thought to aid well-being, improve breathing and lead to more positive emotions). All this combines to make a room with a water feature feel tranquil, fresh and healthy.

You can bring water features into your home by adding small indoor waterfalls, fountains, aquariums or a simple bowl of fresh water refilled daily. If you decide to try an aquarium, it is important to ensure that you set it up and look after it in a way that keeps the fish healthy.

Opposite: A simple water feature is the best place to start. Refresh the water at the start of each day.

Below: This aquarium enhances the room with its calm, tranquil and peaceful energy.

If you prefer something unique, you can make your own water feature. Buy a large glass, metal or ceramic container, an electric water pump and decorative items such as large stones. Place the pump in the container so that the output pipe is above the proposed water level, then arrange the stones so that they hide the pump and provide an attractive form for the water to run across. Plug in and switch on the pump. Play around with the pump and stones until the feature makes the sound you find most calming. You can then add appropriate plants and lilies to your water feature.

Ideally a water feature should be sited in a sunny part of your home so that the sun energizes the water — in feng shui, a water feature is often placed in the east or south-east areas of a home, so that the water is energized by the rising sun in the morning.

Different kinds of water feature will subtly change the energy flow within a room.

water and energy

Water feature	Energy flow	Characteristics
Aquarium	Multi-directional, steady, even, volatile	Choose fish according to the feel you are looking for; quick-moving, colourful fish will be more energizing, while big, slow fish will be more calming
Bowl of fresh water	Multi-directional, slow, even, consistent	Change the water each morning and place the bowl in sunlight for greater effect
Fountain	Up and out, fast, even, fluid	The higher and stronger the fountain, the more powerful its influence
Pond	Multi-directional, slow, even, consistent	Keep a pond alive with plenty of plants, fish, frogs and appropriate pond life
Waterfall	Down, fast, even, fluid	A heavy gushing waterfall will have a powerful influence, whereas a slow trickle will be much more peaceful

salt

According to some evolutionary theory, humans ultimately evolved from sea creatures, giving us a strong primal and evolutionary relationship with sea salt. Most of our body fluids have a salty taste. Salt in the form of sodium is an essential ingredient of our blood and sea salt has a similar energetic frequency to the salt in our bodies. We can therefore use clean sea salt in the home to energetically connect to the sea salt in our bodies and cleanse the energy there.

salt and energy

The most powerful way to benefit from the energy of sea salt is to put a small sachet of it over your navel or in the waistband of your trousers or skirt. This can help you feel more secure and give you a greater feeling of power in your centre. Some people find it also helps with motion sickness. In a similar way, heating up a cup full of salt in a dry pan, then wrapping it in a towel or cloth and placing it over your abdomen can help when you have a stomach upset or diarrhoea. Handle it carefully as the salt can get very hot.

Below: If we think of the sea as our evolutionary mother, both sea water and sea salt carry a strong primal and nurturing energy.

using salt in the home

In your home, small open containers (such as a saucer full of sea salt) are helpful for cleansing the atmosphere and stabilizing the flow of energy through your home. Having a strong *inward-moving, slow, concentrated, consistent* energy, the salt will draw in energy from the room, taking with it any stagnant, stale energy. You could use this to keep the energy of a room that you want to meditate in clear and clean. Sea salt is also valuable in a room that is used for healing or where you want to feel particularly clear-minded.

To help stabilize the energy of your home and make it feel less volatile, try putting two tablespoons of sea salt in a small ramekin and placing it in the north-east and south-west parts of your home. This will calm the energy flow along this potentially less-stable axis. The salt in the dishes needs changing every two months.

Alternatively you can energetically cleanse the atmosphere of a specific part of your home by sprinkling sea salt on the floor before you go to bed and vacuuming it up the next day — make sure you throw it out of your home the following day. This is helpful if you want to clear your home of the residual energy from a negative experience. Perhaps a bad argument or a moment of great stress has left its mark on the atmosphere of a room, and you want to speed up the process of feeling it leave your home.

You could also use sea salt to cleanse a part of your home that you feel might have been affected by a past historical event, or in a place where you or a family member has seen a ghost.

Left: This dish of sea salt helps stabilize and thoroughly cleanse the surrounding atmosphere.

clocks

Clocks add *outward, steady, even, fluid* rhythm and motion to a space. They remind us of time passing and provide a visual reminder of the cycle of the day. A mechanical clock or one with any kind of pendulum will bring greater movement to a room, and the swing of the pendulum has a rhythmic influence on the energy of the space.

clocks in the home

If you fill a room with pendulum clocks, they will all swing together after a while. Any rhythmic cycle encourages other cycles with a similar rhythm to synchronize. For example, women living together often find that their menstrual cycles harmonize. The rhythmic motion of a pendulum will fill your home with a beat that you can tune into. We are made of rhythms — heartbeat, breathing — so the rhythms of life make a big difference to the way we feel.

A regular ticking sound adds sonic rhythm to a room and will help you tune into this beat. You may find that living in a home with rhythm makes it easy to pick up a rhythm of your own, helping you to pace yourself throughout the day and — like dancing to music — pick up greater endurance or march with others to a uniform rhythm.

Clocks are helpful when you want to live a more structured life with greater routine. The rhythm and the visual and sonic marking-out of time passing can help you become more punctual and find a rhythm of moving easily from one activity to another at the correct times throughout the day.

In addition to clocks, you can add more rhythm to your day by eating your meals at exactly the same time every day, and by going to sleep and waking at the same time for a few days. As you do so, you will find that your whole body tunes into these rhythms and you naturally want to eat, sleep and wake up at the same time each day. This can be helpful when you desire greater consistency, assuredness and security in life.

To get the greatest influence from a clock, you should place it in the north-west area of your home, where it will tune in naturally to the evening, late-autumn energy of the heavens.

You can choose from wall-mounted clocks, free-standing clocks and grandfather clocks. Older clocks have more mechanical, metal moving parts and will in theory be better at influencing the energy of a room. An electronic digital clock has the smallest influence.

Below: A pendulum clock brings an energetic rhythm to the room, helping the occupants find their own rhythm.

Opposite: This large, imposing clock makes time the dominant feature of the room. Ideal for punctuality!

sounds

Sounds vibrate the air and, as these vibrations move into your outer energy field, resonate and change your energy. Although you only hear sound with your ears, you experience it through your energy and skin. A deep, loud, bass sound can vibrate your bones in the same way that chanting can. Sounds are a very helpful way to alter your energy and, as a result, can bring about strong changes in your emotions.

sounds and energy

Sound	Energy flow
Wind chimes	Outward, fast, thin, fluid
Bells	Outward, fast, even, volatile
Chanting	Outward, steady, thin, fluid

Right: Hang wind chimes so that the top of the door hits the tag, ringing the chimes each time it is opened.

wind chimes

The sound of a wind chime sends out ripples of energy, which help move and spread out the atmosphere. This can disperse concentrated energy, making it thinner and therefore more relaxing to be in. Typically wind chimes are used to spread out the energy around doors where it can become congested. In addition, the ringing of a wind chime here will help to disperse energy throughout your home.

Wind chimes are only active in terms of moving energy when they chime, so hang them above a door so that the top of the door hits the tag ringing the chimes each time the door is opened. Alternatively, hang them in a windy place so that the wind stimulates the chimes to ring.

bells

The sound of a bell will help distribute energy and send it out to any part of your home where you can hear the sound, because the sound waves carry energy with them. Hand bells are also useful for stirring up stagnant energy. If your home is feeling flat, take a hand bell and ring it in all the corners and anywhere that dust usually collects. The sound waves refresh, and will help get the energy moving again.

Ringing a bell is particularly helpful for sending your own energy out into your home. Hold the bell close to you when you ring it, so that the sound originates from within your own energy field. Think about the dreams you want to project in your mind as you ring the bell. As you do so, the sound waves will ripple through your energy field and into your home, carrying your energy with them.

chanting

Another option is make sounds deep within you and project them into your home by chanting. Chanting is best done in a relatively open, uncluttered space where you can expand your energy.

To move the energy up your body, take in a deep breath and start with the lowest 'aah' sound, moving the vibration up your body by going to a higher-pitched 'aah' sound, then up through the range of 'ooo' and 'mmm' sounds until you reach the top of your head. Once you are comfortable with the sounds, try making 'aah', 'ooo', 'mmm' sounds all in one breath. If you do this several times you will feel a lift in your energy, and a rush of energy to your head. At the same time you will be projecting these sounds and, through them, your energy into your home. Think of positive thoughts to project at the same time.

Above: Bells send sonic energy throughout your home, waking up the energy in every recess.

mirrors and crystals

Mirrors help to redirect and keep energy moving in a fast, fluid way, whereas hanging crystals refract sunlight into the various colours of the rainbow and then spread this energy around a room.

mirrors, crystals and energy

Item	Energy flow
Standard mirrors	Multi-directional, fast, even, fluid
Convex mirrors	Outward, fast, thin, fluid
Crystals	Outward, fast, thin, fluid

mirrors

Mirrors are ideal in dark rooms because they reflect all the available light back into the room, helping to make it more vibrant. You may find that large mirrors improve the atmosphere in a basement room or dark corridor. You can also use mirrors to give a view of either outdoors or of a part of your home, such as a door, that you would not normally be able to see easily.

In small or narrow rooms, large mirrors will give the impression that the room is wider than it really is. Here it is best to hang mirrors on the longer walls to create the impression that the proportions of the room are closer to a square. One or two large mirrors will create a more consistent, open atmosphere, whereas lots of small mirrors can create a crazed, disjointed reflection and therefore a less tranquil atmosphere.

Generally avoid positioning mirrors so that they are directly opposite a door or window, because they will reflect energy straight out of your home again, creating greater congestion and a greater intensity of energy around the door or window. Two mirrors opposite each other risk bouncing energy back and forth, creating a more frantic atmosphere.

Keep mirrors in your bedroom to a minimum, and avoid having a mirror facing your bed, because it can reflect back at you the emotional energy that you release in your dreams. Since mirrors generally speed up the flow of energy, they make the atmosphere too fast for sound sleep.

You can hang a mirror on a wall so that, as you open your front door, you can see round into your home, making the feeling of entering and leaving it a little more secure, while at the same time helping energy flow around the door more easily.

The material of a mirror's frame can influence the feel of a room. Choose softer materials like wood if you want a relaxing atmosphere and a harder material such as metal for a more stimulating feel.

Left: Hanging a convex mirror so that it faces you as you descend the stairs helps disperse and spread energy, creating a greater feeling of harmony.

Below: A crystal spreads sunlight and solar energy throughout a room, and generates a more stimulating area.

convex mirrors

Convex mirrors – round ones with a fish-eye lens – help to disperse energy. They are useful where you want to spread out congested energy. For example, you could hang a convex mirror above the door at the end of a long corridor, or above your front door if your stairs lead straight to it. Alternatively, you could hang the mirror so that it faces you as you descend the stairs.

crystals

Crystals come in the form of clear spheres, teardrops or multi-faceted spheres; they are usually sold with a cord so that you can hang them up. They are best suspended just inside a window or below a skylight. Watch how the sunlight refracts into your room as the sun moves across the sky – reposition the crystal until you feel it is in the ideal position.

Refracting sunlight into a room can help pick up its energy and give the space a more sunny disposition. This helps when you want to feel more vital and uplifted. Too many crystals, though, and the room can feel chaotic and confused.

furniture and bedding

Chairs, tables, beds and bedding are important in feng shui because they contribute to the atmosphere around you while you are seated or sleeping. In the case of chairs, they also define how you sit and therefore how your energy flows while you are in that chair. Tables define how you interact with others, because their shape determines your orientation to other people.

furniture and energy

Furniture and bedding	Energy flow	Characteristics
Tall stools	Up, fast, concentrated, fluid	A tall stool raises you off the ground, exposing you to vertical flowing energy and making it easier to feel alert; as your posture tends to be more erect, energy will rise through your body easily
Large floor cushions	Horizontal and down, slow, thin, consistent	These expose you to more settled energy, making it easier to relax, feel closer to someone and be comfortable; you can adopt a more slanted, pose, encouraging your energy to align with horizontal energy
Round or oval tables	Inward, steady, concentrated, fluid	Round and oval tables enable everyone to see each other and interact easily; this is ideal when you want everyone to get involved in a conversation
Wooden beds	Up, steady, even, fluid	Wood is the ideal material for a bed frame, because it does not distort the local magnetic field; it is softer than metal and contributes to a more calming energy when you sleep
Four-poster beds	Inward, slow, even, consistent	A four-poster bed helps contain the energy around you and is particularly useful if you sleep in a large bedroom with high ceilings where the energy moves quickly

choosing a bed

Sleep is considered carefully in feng shui, because while you sleep you regenerate and heal yourself. Your bed and bedding will have an effect on how well you sleep. Choose a mattress made from natural materials: cotton, wool, straw and hair are preferable to foam and other man-made materials; synthetics carry a static charge and, since this will be inside your energy field, it can eventually make you feel unsettled.

Right: A four-poster bed helps to contain energy.

Furniture and bedding	Energy flow	Characteristics
High beds	Up, steady, even, fluid	A bed that is high off the ground can place you in a more upward, vertical energy flow, which can help you feel imaginative, creative and inspired
Low futons	Horizontal and down, slow, even, consistent	A futon that is set low and close to the ground positions you in a more horizontal flow of energy; this is better for feeling settled, secure and stable
Cotton futons	Multi-directional, slow, even, consistent	Cotton futons are a good choice because they promote harmonious energy flow; use a wooden base to raise the futon off the floor and to air it properly, or put it on any wooden slatted bed base — the firmness will help if you suffer from back problems
Cotton or linen bedding	Multi-directional, slow, even, consistent	It is best to have pure cotton or linen closest to your skin because these materials breathe, which is important as humans can secrete up to 1 litre (1¾ pint) of fluid at night through their skin while sleeping; and these materials do not carry a static charge of electricity

timing

As the energy of the planet goes through its cycles of change, there are times when we find it easier to succeed at certain tasks. The biggest influences on us are the sun and the moon. Using the same ideas about environmental energy and personal change, you will learn here and on the pages that follow how to make the most of the seasons, lunar cycle, equinoxes and solstices.

the seasons and energy

Season	Energy flow
Spring	Up, fast, even, fluid
Summer	Out, fast, even, volatile
Autumn	Inward, steady, concentrated, consistent
Winter	Multi-directional, slow, thin, fluid

the seasons

In a temperate climate we experience what we think of as four seasons, which are marked out by the equinoxes (when the sun is over the equator, and day and night are of equal length) and the solstices (when the sun reaches its highest or lowest point in the sky at noon, resulting in the longest and shortest days). Each season has a distinct environmental atmosphere that we have already experienced many times, depending on our age.

In each season you can tap into the natural energy around you and use it to help you best succeed in your challenges. You can draw on your experience of the seasons to help you plan ahead – perhaps you will be more successful starting a new project in the spring rather than the winter. Use the information below to help deepen your appreciation of how the seasons can influence you.

spring

In the spring we are surrounded by plants actively growing, by the birth of creatures and by the oncoming of warmer weather. This is often seen in feng shui as the beginning of the cycle and the start of the new year. Therefore you should think of this as the ideal time to start new projects, focus on building your career, take on new activities and build up a surge of movement that will carry you forward to fresh challenges.

summer

The summer brings a colourful, hot, fiery phase to the seasons. Nature is in full bloom and everything is in full view. This season is most stimulating for our senses in terms of sounds, smells, tastes, images and touch. It is the time we sunbathe, swim and expose our skin to nature; a time when we can connect sensually with nature. We think of it as the season for self-expression, being outgoing and sociable and bringing

Left: The atmosphere of the autumn is conducive to staying in, cosiness and coming together.

energy to the surface. This is the time to be noticed, enhance your reputation, make friends and reach out for new experiences.

autumn

Now nature is settling down as we move into harvest time. Rather than being a time of growth, this is when fruits are ripening. We are moving into a phase of making the most of what we have and focusing on the quality of life. This is an excellent atmosphere in which to complete projects, find contentment and satisfaction in your work. It is a coming-home energy, when you might find it easier to save and increase your wealth.

winter

The winter is a time of regeneration. This is when the soil prepares for a new growing season. It is a time when everything is quiet on the surface and animals hibernate. For us humans, we can think of it as a period of healing and self-development, getting ready for a new phase in our lives. This is an ideal time to look inward on yourself and see what you can change in order to be more successful during the next year. It is a season associated with sex, conception, objectivity and spirituality.

the lunar cycle

The moon reflects sunlight onto our planet at night and affects the earth's gravitational field, contributing to the rising and falling tides in the seas. It goes through a cycle of almost 30 days, bringing rhythm to the planet, creating an energetic pulse. Some women find that their menstrual cycles harmonize with the lunar cycle, which suggests that the moon has an influence on reproduction.

There is much statistical evidence that the moon influences our behaviour. At the time of a full moon there are more admissions to casualty wards, car accidents increase and the crime rate goes up – all by between 2 and 4 per cent. In addition there are said to be more disturbances among patients in institutions that look after people with mental-health issues.

new moon

At this point in the cycle the lunar energy is quiet, and this makes for a beneficial time to be reflective and think of new ideas and changes that you might want to bring about within yourself. This is a helpful time to feel meditative and contemplative. In addition, the sun and the moon are exerting their gravitational influence from a similar side of the earth, pulling the tides more strongly and creating greater clarity of direction. This encourages a more individual, vertical flow of energy. This is similar to the energy of the north.

lunar cycle and energy

Phase of the moon	Energy flow
New moon	Up and down, slow, even, fluid
Waxing moon	Horizontal, steady, even, fluid
Full moon	Out, fast, even, volatile
Waning moon	Inward, steady, even, fluid

waxing moon

Now the lunar reflection of the sun is rising, and we become more aware of the moon each night. This creates a gentle rise in energy that you can use to help get new projects started and generate fresh ideas. If you have an interesting insight during the new moon, this is an ideal phase to explore ways to put those ideas into action. During this rising tide of lunar energy you can sometimes ride its wave, enabling you to pick up the momentum to take you through the later, quieter waning cycle and new moon. This is similar to the energy of the east.

full moon

Now the moon is on the opposite side of the planet, reflecting sunlight back at us. This spreads the sun's energy and makes the night brighter, as well as creating a gravitational pull from the other side of the planet. This is a helpful time to act on your thoughts, spread your ideas and be more sociable. You may find that you are more successful in attracting people to a social gathering at this time. Generally people feel more lively and outgoing. This is similar to the energy of the south.

waning moon

After the full moon, the moon goes into its waning phase. Here the energy is diminishing and becoming progressively more inward-looking. This is an excellent time to take stock of your life, cherish what you have and explore the practicalities of being efficient and effective. It is an interesting moment to focus on developing your own inner strength and resources. This is similar to the energy of the west.

Above: This full moon has a strong influence on the energy of the planet.

equinoxes and solstices

The equinoxes and solstices are four defining points throughout the year. The winter solstice marks the shortest day of the year; the spring equinox the midpoint when the sun is over the equator; the summer solstice the longest day of the year; and the autumn equinox halfway between the two solstices, when the sun is over the equator again.

times of harmony and change

During the spring and autumn equinoxes every part of the planet experiences sunrise and sunset at almost the same time, because the sun is directly over the equator. On these two days the whole planet resonates with harmony in terms of solar energy. In theory this makes the two equinoxes excellent days to try to understand other people and find common ground. They may be days on which you find it easier to heal differences and move on from past difficulties in relationships.

Below: The sun rising on the spring equinox creates a stimulating, up energy that can help generate greater enthusiasm.

equinoxes, solstices and energy

In this chart the months for the southern hemisphere are given in brackets.

Occasion	Date	Energy flow	Characteristics
Spring equinox	20 or 21 March (September)	Up, fast, even, fluid	Here we are immersed in rising spring energy; this is a traditional time for starting fresh projects and looking at self-improvement
Summer solstice	20 or 21 June (December)	Out, fast, even, volatile	Now we experience the longest, most fiery day of the year with the greatest exposure to the sun's solar energy
Autumn equinox	22 or 23 September (March)	Inward, steady, concentrated, consistent	On this day we experience mid-autumn and a more settling energy; in many cultures this is when the educational season begins
Winter solstice	21 or 22 December (June)	Multi-directional, slow, dispersed, fluid	At this time we witness the shortest day of the year, with the least exposure to the sun's solar energy

The solstices mark the height of summer and winter, corresponding to the longest and shortest days of the year respectively. These are important days because they are times of change. They therefore represent a period of reorientation when we can find new directions. They mark the point when the solar cycle changes and we reach the extreme in terms of energy. This is when you might experience the strongest feelings and perhaps the greatest realizations about yourself.

In terms of energy, the seasons — as defined by the equinoxes and solstices — are similar to the phases of the lunar cycle, except that, whereas the lunar cycle occurs nearly every 30 days and just over 12 times a year, the solar cycle takes one whole year.

In feng shui, the beginning of the year is considered to be halfway between the winter solstice and the spring equinox, when spring starts — this is when environmental energy begins to rise.

room makeovers with eight-direction energy

In this last part of the book you will explore each of the eight directions in detail and will discover how the energy of each one relates to your emotional energy and how you can make specific changes in your home to create a different atmosphere and mood (see pages 122–137). In addition you will see how you can alter the energy in each room to encompass the atmosphere of one of the eight directions. This is where you will learn more about the practical application of feng shui and will actually see it in action.

northern energy makeover

Try these suggestions if you want to bring this winter, night-time energy into a room. They will be most effective if the room is in the north of your home, but can also be applied if it is in the west, north-west, east or south-east part of your home or if the windows face one of these directions. The aim is an atmosphere that feels multi-directional, slow, thin and fluid, with the northern qualities of being flexible, quiet, dark, flowing, moonlit, starry, mysterious, tranquil and regenerative.

sleeping

If practical, turn your bed so that the top of your head points north (hold a compass over your bed to find north). This will bring in more northern energy through the crown chakra, or activity centre at the top of your head, while you sleep. Northern energy is ideal for deep sleep and may also help you direct more internal energy into healing overnight.

sitting

Try arranging the chairs in your home so that at least one faces north. Ideally it will also have its back to a corner or wall and a view of the whole room and (if appropriate) the windows and doors. When you sit in this chair you will find it easier to relax and will absorb more northern energy.

colours

To create a wintry, moonlit atmosphere in a room, try using a cream colour. You could also bring in elements of shiny black to create a more watery feel. Use large blocks of plain colour, rather than patterns or anything busy. Choose hues that help you feel serene and tranquil.

materials

Materials that are hard and cool are ideal for creating that winter feel. Try stone, wooden or metal surfaces. Rugs or carpets slow the flow of energy, making it harder to get that big, free-flowing night sensation. You will find that large blocks of the same surface work best at creating a northern atmosphere. If the northern part of your home is dark, use shiny surfaces to reflect the natural light and keep this area alive.

lighting

Think of a big, full moon for lighting ideas. To create this effect, your lighting should be indirect and diffused, so you could reflect it off a wall or ceiling. Another option is to diffuse the light through misted glass or a paper screen, producing a muted cream glow.

surfaces

Explore ways to keep a room with a northern feel as open and free from clutter as possible, so that you find it easier to feel spiritual, objective and meditative. See if you can move items into storage so that this room has a feeling of space and openness.

special features

A large mirror can make a room appear twice the size and encourages a big, open feel. Paper screens and lampshades help to create a clean winter atmosphere.

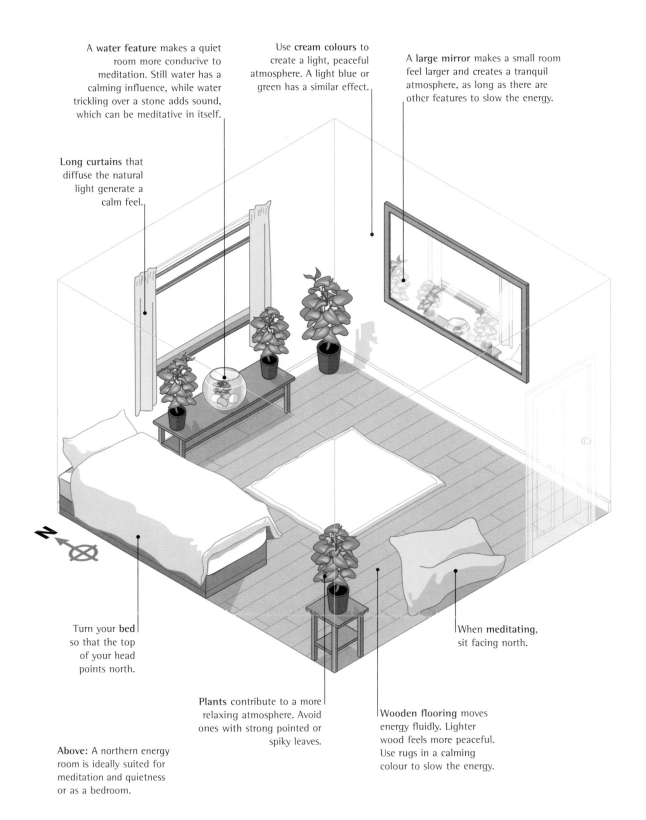

A **water feature** makes a quiet room more conducive to meditation. Still water has a calming influence, while water trickling over a stone adds sound, which can be meditative in itself.

Use **cream colours** to create a light, peaceful atmosphere. A light blue or green has a similar effect.

A **large mirror** makes a small room feel larger and creates a tranquil atmosphere, as long as there are other features to slow the energy.

Long curtains that diffuse the natural light generate a calm feel.

Turn your **bed** so that the top of your head points north.

When **meditating**, sit facing north.

Plants contribute to a more relaxing atmosphere. Avoid ones with strong pointed or spiky leaves.

Wooden flooring moves energy fluidly. Lighter wood feels more peaceful. Use rugs in a calming colour to slow the energy.

Above: A northern energy room is ideally suited for meditation and quietness or as a bedroom.

north-eastern energy makeover

To bring more of this late-winter, early-morning energy into your being, try the following features. Being in the north-eastern part of your home or facing north-east will harness this energy most, but it can also work if the room is in the southern, south-western, western or north-western parts of your home, or if the windows face one of these directions. The aim is to create a fast, concentrated and fluid atmosphere that feels multi-directional and up, with the crisp, clean, clear, sharp, quick, hard and cold qualities of north-eastern energy.

sleeping

Use a compass to turn your bed so that the top of your head points north-east, to recharge yourself with more of this energy overnight. In some people this increases the risk of poor sleep and even nightmares; if so, choose east instead.

sitting

Look out for a place in your home where you can sit facing north-east and soak up more of this energy through the front of your body. The most powerful location will be where most of the room is in front of you. Wander around your home with a compass so that you can easily locate the ideal position.

colours

Try brilliant white with touches of yellow and purple to re-create the early-morning, mountain atmosphere. Ideally the room will remind you of a fresh, crisp winter's day with snow and frost lying on the ground.

materials

Stone is ideal to create a north-eastern atmosphere. Slate and other cold, grey stones also capture the mountain atmosphere. Alternatively, use white stone to mirror the appearance of snow.

lighting

Bright lighting that is masked can create the impression of the sun about to come up on the horizon. Consider lights behind a solid screen, shielded wall lights and lighting set behind cabinet plinths or solid discs.

surfaces

Hard, pristine, smooth, clear surfaces add to a north-eastern atmosphere. Again white or grey stone has a mountain feel. Shiny surfaces speed up the energy further, so a marble floor or countertop enhances the effect.

special features

Try creating a rockery in the north-eastern part of your home or room. This could be an assortment of interesting rocks arranged in an absorbing way. You can use this as a focus for meditation or contemplation when you want to be decisive, clear-minded and motivated.

Another option is to set up a tray or shallow box with gravel that you can rake into different patterns, whenever you want to empty your mind and let new ideas float in to help you find a fresh direction in life. You can also create a bigger version with a gravel pit in a secluded part of your garden. Sit facing north-east with the gravel in front of you. Think about the issue that troubles you, then mentally put it to one side while you totally absorb yourself in raking the gravel. As you do this, let your subconscious work on the problem for you. Move the rake in a natural, easy manner, letting the patterns in the gravel come out freely. Once you become mesmerized by the gravel, you may find that a solution pops into your head.

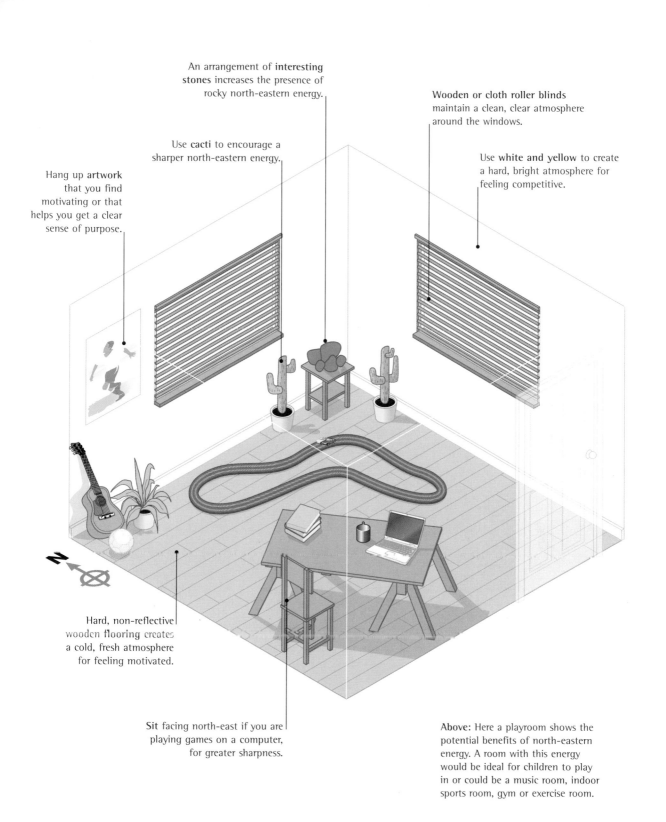

An arrangement of **interesting stones** increases the presence of rocky north-eastern energy.

Wooden or cloth roller blinds maintain a clean, clear atmosphere around the windows.

Use **cacti** to encourage a sharper north-eastern energy.

Use **white and yellow** to create a hard, bright atmosphere for feeling competitive.

Hang up **artwork** that you find motivating or that helps you get a clear sense of purpose.

Hard, non-reflective wooden flooring creates a cold, fresh atmosphere for feeling motivated.

Sit facing north-east if you are playing games on a computer, for greater sharpness.

Above: Here a playroom shows the potential benefits of north-eastern energy. A room with this energy would be ideal for children to play in or could be a music room, indoor sports room, gym or exercise room.

eastern energy makeover

To bring more eastern, springtime, sunrise energy into your being, try the following suggestions. This eastern bathroom will naturally have an upward, fresh, morning atmosphere. The makeover can also be applied, though, if the room is in the south-eastern, southern or northern parts of your home, or if the windows face one of these directions. The aim is to create a room where the atmosphere feels upward, fast, concentrated and fluid, with the new, fresh, electric and active qualities of eastern energy.

sleeping
Reposition your bed so that the top of your head points east and to the sunrise, to replenish your body with more upward energy overnight. A wooden bed frame and space around your head will further help.

sitting
Watch where the sun rises over the horizon, to establish a place where you can sit facing east, with the room and (if possible) the doors and windows in front of you. You will be facing the morning sun as it appears on the horizon. To increase the feeling of upward energy, sit on a stool or high, upright chair.

colours
The colour that is associated with the east is the green that you see on a new springtime bud or leaf. This is a light mint-green that creates a fresh, upward atmosphere related to new life and the morning.

materials
To create an eastern atmosphere in your home, use wood — a light, living material that encourages energy to flow upwards and brings energy into the room. Wood may apply to floors, furniture or walls, but to be effective it needs to be solid. Bare wood will have the greatest influence on the atmosphere of a room. A natural wax finish or oil seasoning will enable the energy of the wood to interact with the energy of the room.

lighting
Uplighting moves the energy up in a room. This is ideal when you want a room to feel taller. Uplighters are particularly helpful under a heavy beam or where the ceiling slopes down.

surfaces
Polished horizontal surfaces, such as a polished wooden floor, reflect energy upward, giving the room a rising energy. This also applies to large wooden tables and other big surfaces such as worktops.

special features
Plants that grow up encourage energy to move upwards in a room and contribute to a rising, up, eastern atmosphere. A large number of growing plants will improve the air quality and give the space a green colour, engendering a springtime feeling and generally enlivening the whole space.

Strong vertical forms in a room help to make the space feel taller, encouraging an upward, vertical movement of energy. Vertical stripes and blinds, a hatstand, a tall lampstand and stools all enhance a rising flow of energy.

To leave your home feeling fresher in terms of its atmosphere — similar to the feeling after a storm — and to bring in a sense of thunder, try ringing a large gong so that the sound vibrates throughout your home. This will stir up the energy in all the deepest recesses.

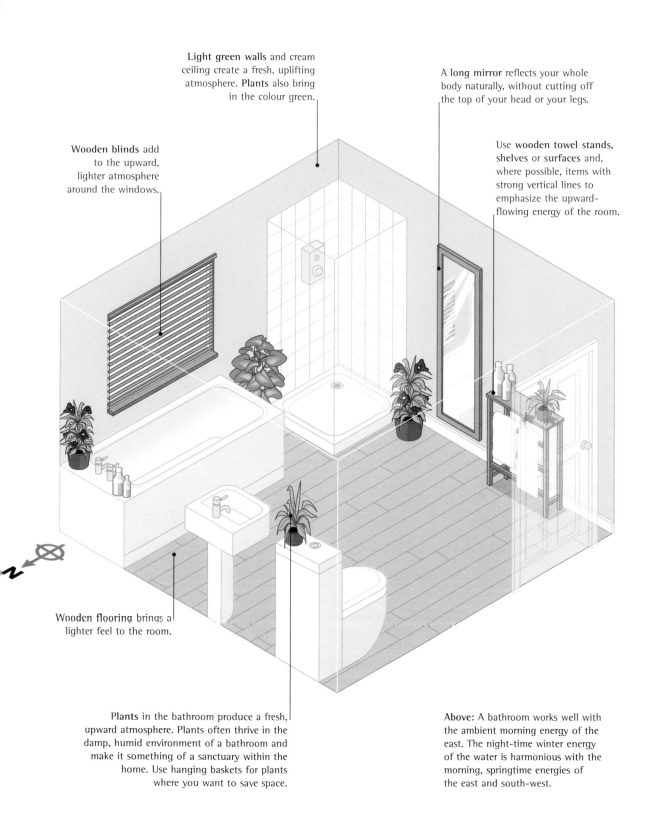

Light green walls and cream ceiling create a fresh, uplifting atmosphere. Plants also bring in the colour green.

A long mirror reflects your whole body naturally, without cutting off the top of your head or your legs.

Wooden blinds add to the upward, lighter atmosphere around the windows.

Use wooden towel stands, shelves or surfaces and, where possible, items with strong vertical lines to emphasize the upward-flowing energy of the room.

Wooden flooring brings a lighter feel to the room.

Plants in the bathroom produce a fresh, upward atmosphere. Plants often thrive in the damp, humid environment of a bathroom and make it something of a sanctuary within the home. Use hanging baskets for plants where you want to save space.

Above: A bathroom works well with the ambient morning energy of the east. The night-time winter energy of the water is harmonious with the morning, springtime energies of the east and south-west.

south-eastern energy makeover

A kitchen is perfect for the energy of the south-east. This kitchen makeover can also be applied when the room is in the eastern, southern or northern parts of your home, or if the windows face one of these directions. The aim is to create a room where the atmosphere feels upward, fast, concentrated and fluid, with the new, fresh, electric and active qualities of eastern energy. Bring more south-eastern, late-spring, morning energy into your body with the following suggestions.

sleeping

Watch the sun rise through the morning and turn your bed so that the top of your head points south-east to the morning sun, to encourage more of that energy to fill your body overnight. If practical, keep the sides of your bed away from the walls; even consider having the top of your head away from a wall, to enable the energy around it to flow easily and capture the feeling of the south-eastern wind energy.

sitting

Watch the morning sun to find a place where you can rest facing south-east, with the room, doors and windows in front of you so that you receive the sun's energy as it rises through the morning.

colours

Use a sky-blue to give your home the feel of a windy, morning sky. Alternatively, a dark green — similar to the colour of more mature plants — will capture the atmosphere of the morning and of spring turning to summer.

materials

A home made from wood will have a light, upward atmosphere than can help you take in more south-eastern energy. This will be most powerful when the wood is exposed to the interior of the home, creating a smell of wood; this applies to floors, furniture, panelled walls, exposed beams and worktops.

lighting

Try using lights that shine up a wall or onto the ceiling to move energy upwards more easily. As this style of lighting requires the beam to reflect off the walls or ceiling, white or light-coloured surfaces will work best. Placing a light behind a plant that is moving in the breeze will create moving shadows, helping to emphasize the feeling of wind and movement.

surfaces

A polished wooden floor, table or worktop will reflect energy up, helping to create a stronger flow of upward energy. To be most effective, keep these surfaces clear. This will also encourage a freer movement of energy to capture the south-eastern feeling of wind.

special features

A flowing water feature increases the movement in a room, giving it a more south-eastern feel. Ideally this should have an upward component: it could be a fountain or something that resembles a bubbling spring.

To fill your home with south-eastern energy, open all the windows on a sunny spring morning and let the wind blow fresh energy through it. A well-ventilated home generally has a more energetic feel.

Plenty of plants will encourage a late-springtime atmosphere within your home and bring in a more upward-moving, natural feel.

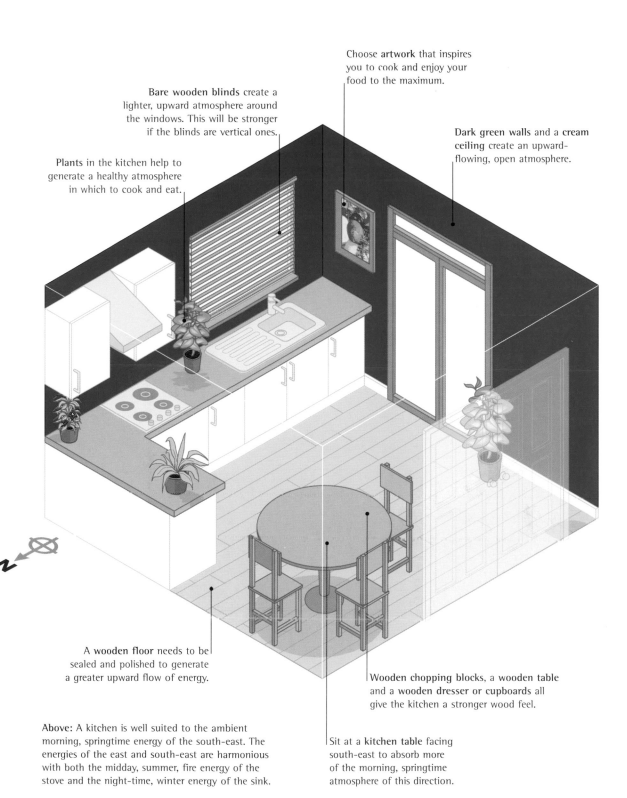

Choose **artwork** that inspires you to cook and enjoy your food to the maximum.

Bare wooden blinds create a lighter, upward atmosphere around the windows. This will be stronger if the blinds are vertical ones.

Dark green walls and a **cream ceiling** create an upward-flowing, open atmosphere.

Plants in the kitchen help to generate a healthy atmosphere in which to cook and eat.

A **wooden floor** needs to be sealed and polished to generate a greater upward flow of energy.

Wooden chopping blocks, a wooden table and a **wooden dresser or cupboards** all give the kitchen a stronger wood feel.

Above: A kitchen is well suited to the ambient morning, springtime energy of the south-east. The energies of the east and south-east are harmonious with both the midday, summer, fire energy of the stove and the night-time, winter energy of the sink.

Sit at a **kitchen table** facing south-east to absorb more of the morning, springtime atmosphere of this direction.

southern energy makeover

You will absorb more southern, summer, midday energy into your body by including the following features in your home. This makeover will be most effective in the southern part of your home, but can also be applied if the room is in the eastern, south-eastern, south-western or north-eastern parts of your home, or if the windows face one of these directions. The aim is to create an atmosphere that is outward, fast, even, volatile and brings in more of the summer, fiery qualities of being hot, bright, radiant, expansive, shimmering and vibrant.

sleeping
Look to see where the sun is at its midday, highest point and work out if you can turn your bed so that the top of your head points in that direction, to absorb more southern energy overnight.

sitting
Use the same method to find a place in your home where you can sit facing south, with as much of the room in front of you as possible. Ideally you will also be able to see the doors and windows from this position.

colours
Sunny, fiery reds, purples and oranges capture the summer, midday energy of the south. These strong colours need to be used with care if they are not to be overwhelming. Intense colours can work well in large rooms with high ceilings, but may be too overpowering for a small room, leading to a stressful atmosphere. In a small room, try touches of these brighter colours against a lighter background.

materials
Instead of materials being specific to the fire energy of the south, sunlight best captures this energy. A home that has plenty of exposure to the sun, and big, open windows letting the solar influence in, will have a wealth of southern energy.

lighting
Bright lighting resembles the sunny energy of the south. You could use direct lighting, and in particular spotlights, to direct high-intensity beams of light on a specific place.

surfaces
The energy of the south can be enhanced by glazed surfaces, such as glazed tiles or pottery. Surfaces that are reflective and uneven spread energy outward around the home, adding to the fiery southern atmosphere.

special features
Candles help to bring more fire energy into a room. To be effective in a larger room, several candles may need to be grouped together. Place the candles in the southern part of your home or room for maximum effect.

A real fire will bring greater fire energy into a room. A fireplace combines convected heat (the kind generated by a radiator) with radiated heat (as produced by the sun). This gives more of a feeling that the sun is in the room.

You may be able to position mirrors so that you can reflect the sunlight coming into a room on into another part of it. This intensifies the presence of southern energy. Another way to achieve this is to hang a crystal so that it refracts sunlight into the darker corners of a room.

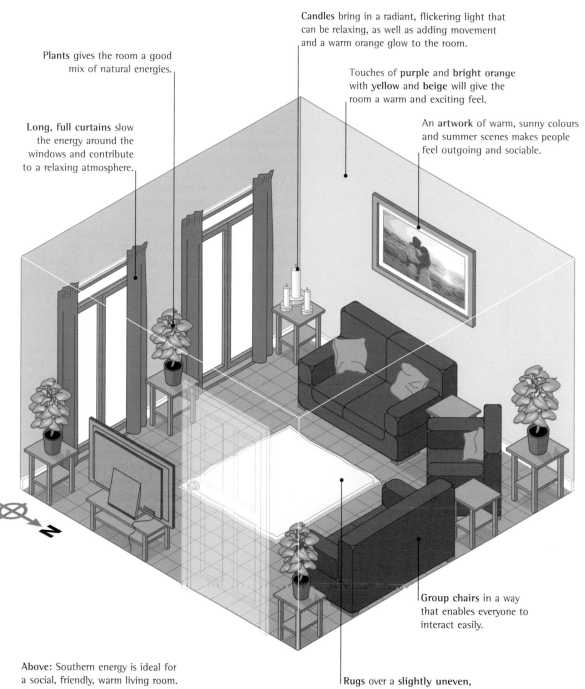

Candles bring in a radiant, flickering light that can be relaxing, as well as adding movement and a warm orange glow to the room.

Plants gives the room a good mix of natural energies.

Long, full curtains slow the energy around the windows and contribute to a relaxing atmosphere.

Touches of **purple** and **bright orange** with **yellow** and **beige** will give the room a warm and exciting feel.

An **artwork** of warm, sunny colours and summer scenes makes people feel outgoing and sociable.

Group chairs in a way that enables everyone to interact easily.

Above: Southern energy is ideal for a social, friendly, warm living room. The midday summer atmosphere will help create a room that is conducive to entertainment and lively conversations.

Rugs over a **slightly uneven, tiled** or **wooden floor** combine a more fiery energy with a softer settled atmosphere.

south-western energy makeover

When you want to absorb more south-western, late-summer, afternoon energy into your body, include the following features in your home. The makeover can also be applied if the room is in the southern, western, north-western or north-eastern parts of your home, or if the windows face one of these directions. The intention is to produce an atmosphere that is downward, steady, even and fluid, while bringing in more of the descending, settling, earthy, warm, waning, soft and ripening late-summer, afternoon qualities.

sleeping

Watch the sun in the afternoon to see its direction when it is in the south-west. To absorb more of its energy in this phase of its cycle, turn your bed so that the top of your head points to the afternoon sun.

sitting

Similarly, find a chair you can sit in (with as much of the room in front of you as possible) so in which you face south-west and the afternoon sun. To accentuate the south-western feel, sit on a low chair or large cushion.

colours

Earthy browns, beiges, dull reds and faded oranges capture the energy of the south-west. These colours work well in rooms that you want to feel settled and relaxed, such as a living room or bedroom. Natural woods, rough clay, brown leather and dyed fabrics can also be used to bring these hues into the room.

materials

Fabrics, clay, soft stone such as limestone, leather and wool all help to slow down the energy in a home and contribute to a south-western atmosphere. Soft chairs, plump sofas, curtains, woollen rugs and big cushions can all be used to enhance this energy, making a room more cosy and intimate.

lighting

To bring the energy in a room down, try placing soft lighting on the floor or on a low table in a corner. This might be a table lamp with a shade in rust colours, a lamp set into an orange salt crystal or candles.

surfaces

Ideally surfaces should be matt and should absorb vertical downward-flowing energy. Terracotta floors, bare plaster walls and carpets help create a south-western feel to a room. To get a bare plaster effect, you can mix colour into the plaster before applying it or leave it undyed in soft, natural tones, but you will have to coat the bare plaster walls with a clear sealant for durability.

special features

Artists' charcoal broken into small pieces and put in an open clay bowl increases south-western energy. This will be most effective when placed in the south-western part of your home.

A yellow flowering plant in a clay container produces strong south-western energy and is helpful in the south-western corner of a room or that part of your home. Similarly, plants with big, floppy leaves in this section of your home bring in more of this slow, downward energy.

Artwork that helps you feel relaxed — and in the mood to sit down and eat — is ideal. Obvious examples are scenes of food growing on the land and still-lifes; however, something more abstract or contemporary works just as well.

Earthy south-western colours are **yellow, brown, beige** and **burnt orange**. These tones are pleasant for a harmonious eating atmosphere.

Thick, heavy curtains encourage a softer feel. They are ideal on cold winter nights and help make the space feel cosy and comfortable.

Matt, **terracotta floors** will absorb vertical downward-flowing energy.

Plants with big, floppy leaves encourage the energy to move slowly and horizontally, as well as keep the energy close to the ground.

An **oval** or **round table** enables a group of friends or large family to interact easily. Facing the sunny, southern directions is generally enlivening, whereas facing one of the quieter, northern directions is calming.

Above: South-western energy produces a comfortable atmosphere for dining. The afternoon, late-summer environment creates a settled feel that is ideal for enjoying each other's company and for taking time to relish a meal.

western energy makeover

To take in more western, autumnal, sunset energy into your body, try bringing the following features into your home. This makeover can also be used if the room is in the south-western, north-eastern, north-western or northern parts of your home, or if the windows face one of these directions. The aim is to produce an atmosphere that is inward, steady, concentrated and consistent, while bringing in the sunset, autumn qualities of completion, the harvest, reflection, romance and playfulness.

sleeping
Make a point of observing the setting sun and note its direction in your bedroom. Turn your bed so that the top of your head points in the same direction: west on a compass. You will now absorb more western, autumn energy overnight.

sitting
Using the same process, find a chair to sit in facing west. To capture a powerful position, make sure that the room is in front of you and that you can see the windows and doors. An armchair with a tall back will help you contain your energy, contributing to a greater inward-energy flow as described by the sunset energy of the west.

colours
Sunset colours best describe western energy. They could include pink, white, grey and maroon. These colours would be particularly good in a western room or anywhere you want to benefit from the attributes of the west. Grey can be a difficult hue in countries with long, dark winters, because it can feel depressing, so instead you could use white.

materials
Metal is the material associated with the west. To be effective in terms of encouraging an inward flow of energy, the surface should be matt, textured and porous. This can be achieved with bare cast iron, or cast iron seasoned with oil to prevent rusting or painted with a matt finish. Shiny metals such as chrome and stainless steel reflect energy, capturing the image of a lake.

lighting
One or two spotlights in a room, highlighting a specific feature, produce an inward-flowing, sunset feel. Ideally the source should produce a circular pool of light on a wall — perhaps lighting a painting — while resembling the sun just above the horizon.

surfaces
A room with matt, textured, hard surfaces — a rough stone floor or cast-iron fixtures such as a wood-burning stove — encourages more metal energy. Cast-iron plant pots and containers are another way to increase the presence of this autumn sunset energy in a room. A horizontal reflective surface, such as a glass table-top, can bring in more of the mirror-like quality of a lake that is associated with western energy.

special features
An arrangement of fading leaves or a maroon flowering plant in a cast-iron container will bring in more of an autumnal, sunset atmosphere. For the greatest effect, place them in the west part of your home or room.

A round table helps to contain the energy of the people sitting there, making it easier to have more focused conversations. Use a round table whenever you want to experience more of the metal energy of the west.

Below: A room with western energy makes for a relaxing but playful bedroom. The sunset, autumnal western atmosphere encourages feelings of contentment and helps you feel more romantic at bedtime.

Pink walls and a **white ceiling** accentuate the romantic, fun aspect of the west.

Curtains that are billowing, frilly or lacy help to create a more fun bedroom atmosphere.

Sleep with the **top of your head pointing west** to emphasize the fun, romantic, playful side of your relationship.

Use **artwork** that helps you feel romantic and playful. This might be in the form of paintings, sculptures or photographs.

Fresh **pink** or **red** **flowers** or **flowering plants** further enhance the western energy.

Carpets slow down the energy and contribute to a cosier, softer atmosphere.

Choose a **bed** with a **wooden frame** and a **mattress made of natural materials**, such as cotton wadding, horsehair or straw. A traditional futon has a cotton cover and is filled with cotton wadding; use it on top of a wooden slatted base or bed.

north-western energy makeover

If you need more north-western, late-autumn, evening energy in your body, use the following features to bring more of that energy into your home. The suggestions will be more effective in the north-western part of your home, but will also work in the south-western, north-eastern, western or northern parts of your home, or where the windows face one of these directions. The intention is to create an inward, slow, concentrated and consistent atmosphere, while bringing in more qualities of preparation, intuition, experience, responsibility, honesty and respect.

sleeping

Use a compass to establish in which direction north-west lies in your bedroom: hold your compass over your bed so that you can clearly see which way you need to turn it to ensure the top of your head points north-west when you sleep.

sitting

Again using a compass, find a chair that can be placed with its back to a wall or corner so that, when seated, you look out into the room while facing north-west. You might find this easiest by holding the compass over the seat of the chair.

colours

Evening, autumn-changing-to-winter colours bring more north-western energy into a room. These include white, grey and silver. White captures the colour of an early frost or snow seen through the evening light. Silver can most easily be achieved through the use of stainless-steel stoves, hobs, refrigerators, furniture, taps, splashbacks, sinks or baths.

materials

Metal is the material associated with the north-west. To bring more north-western, silver energy into a room, look for finishes that are not overtly shiny. For example, brushed stainless steel has a dull finish that captures the colour, without reflecting energy. You are aiming to introduce items that help your own energy move inward and develop greater inner strength.

lighting

Diffused lighting on a single wall can re-create that evening feeling within a room. This can be achieved with a single light or a series of wall lights that shield the beam from the room and reflect it off a white wall.

surfaces

An ordered room suggests the presence of north-western energy. Surfaces could be made of linear wooden planks, parquet or evenly laid tiles. Repeating patterns in fabric or wallpaper further emphasize the orderly atmosphere associated with the evening north-western energy.

special features

A clock carries the energy of the north-west, because it adds rhythm and structure to a room. The effect is increased if the clock has metal parts or a metal face — white and silver are the ideal colours. The rhythmic ticking sound helps to give a room greater rhythm and can enable you to feel more organized. Even more effective is buying a clock with a pendulum, because this will add visual rhythm to the room. A clock is most effective when placed in the north-western part of your home or room.

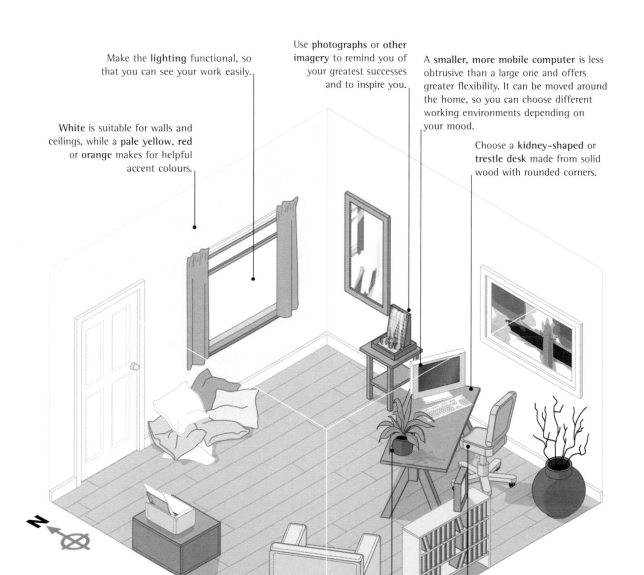

Make the **lighting** functional, so that you can see your work easily.

Use **photographs** or **other imagery** to remind you of your greatest successes and to inspire you.

A **smaller, more mobile computer** is less obtrusive than a large one and offers greater flexibility. It can be moved around the home, so you can choose different working environments depending on your mood.

White is suitable for walls and ceilings, while a **pale yellow, red** or **orange** makes for helpful accent colours.

Choose a **kidney-shaped** or **trestle desk** made from solid wood with rounded corners.

A **stone** or **wooden floor** helps the energy to flow easily and works well for an office environment.

Find a **chair** that is adjustable in height and seat angle, so that you can tilt the seat so that your back feels centred over your lumbar vertebrae.

Sitting facing into the room within sight of the door and windows while facing north-west is most powerful.

Plants reduce the effects of the electromagnetic fields that surround electrical equipment. **Place them near your computer, fax, photocopier and printer.** Healthy, growing plants also clean the air.

Above: A north-western atmosphere is ideal for a home office. The evening, late-autumn atmosphere encourages feelings of control, organization and responsibility. It brings the benefits of wisdom and experience to your work.

glossary

aura: an energy field that surrounds any life form; it can be photographed using a process called Kirlian photography; with practice, people can also feel or see someone's aura

cardinal directions: the four main points of the compass — north, east, south and west

chakra: an activity centre in the body through which energy flows

concepts: ideas, principles and theories developed by human beings to help explain the world we live in

the eight directions: eight compass directions are commonly used in feng shui, being north, south, east and west, along with the four directions in between — north-east, south-east, south-west and north-west

eight-direction house map: a transparency with the eight directions marked out, which can be placed over any house plan and turned to show which direction each part of the home faces

energy field: a subtle charge of electromagnetic electricity that flows through the body and is thought to be influenced by a person's thoughts and emotions

environmental energy: an energy that flows through the universe, primarily stimulated by the stars and the sun in our solar system; this energy flows along the surface of our planet (depending on the landscape) and ultimately influences the energy in a home

feng shui: the study of the way in which humans interact with their environment

five elements: five types of environmental energy that are similar to the atmosphere of five different times of the year or day

I Ching: the Book of Changes, one of the oldest Chinese classic texts, which employs a system of divination to offer insights into a reader's situation

inner life coach: a voice in your head, feelings about yourself or your own self-image

intuition: knowing instinctively what to do, based on a feeling that may have been influenced by past experiences

life coaching: tuition in the art of living to help people do more with their lives

meridian: a path in the body along which energy flows

psychological energy: energy that flows through the human body and has been influenced by, or can influence, the state of a person's mind

transformation: a process of change and evolution that carries you forward throughout your life

translation: the process of changing yourself from one state to another; for example, translating yourself from being unhealthy to healthy, poor to rich, single to married

trigram: a series of three parallel lines used in divination, according to the *I Ching (Book of Changes)*

volatile: liable to change rapidly

yin and yang: adjectives used to describe everything we know — yin and yang are complementary opposites and literally describe the shady side of the mountain (yin) and the sunny side (yang)

index

acknowledgements

author acknowledgements

I would like to acknowledge all those people who have most influenced my energy over the years: Dragana, Christopher, Alexander, Nicholas, Michael, Melanie, Adam, Mum and close friend Jeremy. A special thanks to all my feng shui clients, students and colleagues who have helped shape my understanding of feng shui. I have greatly enjoyed working with everyone at the Feng Shui Society. My heartfelt gratitude also goes to William Spear, who first introduced me to feng shui.

Executive Editor Sandra Rigby
Editor Amy Corbett
Executive Art Editor Penny Stock
Designer Barbara Zuniga
Illustrator Sudden Impact Media
Picture Librarian and Researcher Taura Riley
Production Assistant Hannah Burke

special Photography:
©Octopus Publishing Group Limited/Russell Sadur

other Photography:
Alamy/David White 118; The Garden Picture Library/Linda Burgess 79; WoodyStock 102
Corbis UK Ltd/Arcaid/Richard Powers 90; Paul A. Souders 89; Pixland 37
Getty Images/Anders Rising 107; David Lees 71; DEA / C. SAPPA   48; Francesco Bittichesu 94; Justin Pumfrey 43; Ken Hayden 97; Maria Spann 62; Michael Krasowitz 67; Mitsushi Okada 53; Philip and Karen Smith 18; Stuart O'Sullivan 68; T Schmidt 54; Tariq Dajani 8; Victoria Pearson 73; Wide Group 20
Loupe Images/Ryland, Peters & Small 29, 88
NASA Goddard Space Flight Centre 117
Octopus Publishing Group Limited 38, 59; Paul Bricknell 21, 31; Russell Sadur 76, 111
Photolibrary/Edmund Sumner 99; Garden Picture Library/Flora Press 100; Helen King 56; Ian O'Leary 17; Pixland 30; Sean Miller 115; Thomas Patrice 113
Royalty-Free Images/Corbis 36; Getty images 25, 52
Shutterstock/Camilo Torres 65; coko 4; Dainis Derics 109; forestpath 16; Matt Ragen 50; Robert Nolan 92; Stephen Coburn 106; Yuri Arcurs 61.

about the author

consultations and courses
I am available to help with feng shui consultations for your home, office or workplace. These can be arranged with a visit or we can work together via emails and telephone.
I run courses and am available for one-to-one tuition. These courses range from an introduction to feng shui to a full practitioner training.
Please visit my web site for articles and further information.

books by Simon Brown
The Feng Shui Bible, Godsfield Press,
ISBN 978-1-841-81251-9
The Secrets of Face Reading, Godsfield Press,
ISBN 978-1-841-81324-0
Feng Shui in a Weekend, Hamlyn,
ISBN 978-0-600-60378-8
Practical Feng Shui, Cassell Illustrated,
ISBN 978-0-706-37634-0
Practical Wabi Sabi, Carroll & Brown,
ISBN 978-1-904-76055-9
Modern Day Macrobiotics, Carroll & Brown,
ISBN 978-1-904-76024-5
The Healer, O Books/John Hunt Publishing,
ISBN 978-1-84694-205-1

contact details
Simon G. Brown
email: simon@chienergy.co.uk
website: www.chienergy.co.uk
tel: +44 (0) 20 7431 9897